MADE IN HEREFORDSHIRE

Inspiring recipes using the very best Herefordshire produce

Photopia Photography

Made in Herefordshire
www.recipesmadehere.co.uk
Published by Photopia Photography, Copyright © Photopia Photography.
www.photopiaphotography.co.uk
First published 2013

Designed by p and r design
www.pandrdesign.com

Sponsored and Edited by Jo Hilditch

Illustrations by Mister Charlesworth

Printed in Herefordshire by Orphans Press Ltd

Press and PR by The Seed Group

ISBN 978-0-9927021-0-6

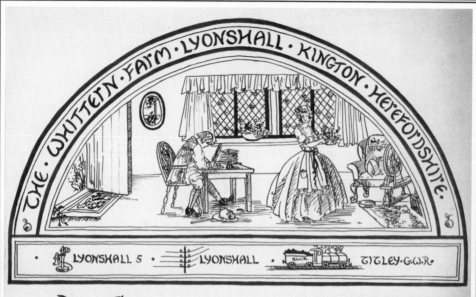

THE · WHITTERN · FARM · LYONSHALL · KINGTON · HEREFORDSHIRE.

· LYONSHALL 5 · LYONSHALL · TITLEY · G.W.R.

Dear Sir.

Will you help the British Farmer?

and at the same time

help yourself

by buying

Farms and

Home-made Produce

direct

from the

Homestead.

Foreword By Jo Hilditch

Promoting the food and drink of Herefordshire is in my blood. In the early 1900s, my great-grandmother was so proud of the fruit, vegetables, meat and eggs she produced on her 'homestead' that she regularly sent one of her farm boys on the train from Titley to the markets in Birmingham and London with baskets overflowing with produce. She was fortunate enough to have 'Lyonshall 5' as her telephone number meaning that she could be contacted relatively easily for remote orders. Now, with advances in technology, just a couple of clicks are required to buy on-line. Nearly 100 years later, here we are, making the same promises as those of my great-grandmother and although our sense of style may have changed (see her own hand-drawn advertisement opposite) our sentiment has not.

Herefordshire is a beautiful county and it is populated with epicureans who continue to make our experiences ever better year on year. Our local food industry is made up of both big and small producers, and we all work together to provide what our customers need, both in and out of the county. That common purpose is visible in this book. From publicans and mixologists, to food producers and cider makers, from wonderful outdoor enamelware suppliers to edible flower growers, the people who have shared their recipes here all love food, especially the food they can find on their doorstep.

Reading through the recipes and the short quotes included here, I am fascinated to discover that whether the contributors are third- or fourth-generation county people or have only arrived in Herefordshire in the last few years, they all believe that their bit of the county is best. This obviously means that Herefordshire is some kind of Arcadia! And it is true: our landscape is staggeringly beautiful – I never tire of the patchwork of ancient woodlands and the undulating parklands, nor the more modern vibrant yellow of oilseed rape, the changing colours of our many arable crops, the different fruits scattered across the county and the animals that graze on wide green pastures or in the shade of our large indigenous oaks.

It is a pleasure to work with the people too; the spirit of co-operation, friendliness and open-minded adventure that our locals possess has made this book a joy to put together. Even those who couldn't offer a recipe showed great support and unflagging encouragement in this project, which at times seemed an insurmountable challenge. It is this shared sense that we are all in it together that makes the difference; everyone needs to do their bit in making eating and drinking a better experience. For my own part, I farm on both a large and a small scale but it is the pleasure of seeing someone's eyes light up when they taste our British Cassis that is probably my finest reward.

Our photographers, as perfectionists of their trade, have taken such time and care over every shot in the book. Their passionate belief in Herefordshire food is reflected in the originality and the detail of the recipes they have helped pull together, and the variety of their ingredients. It is also a matter of pride that we have kept all other aspects of the book's production in the county. The printers and the designers are local too and have been as committed to the outcome as we have. So thank you to everyone involved – without you all it wouldn't have come together.

Watch out for Made in Herefordshire Part II – there may be more to come…

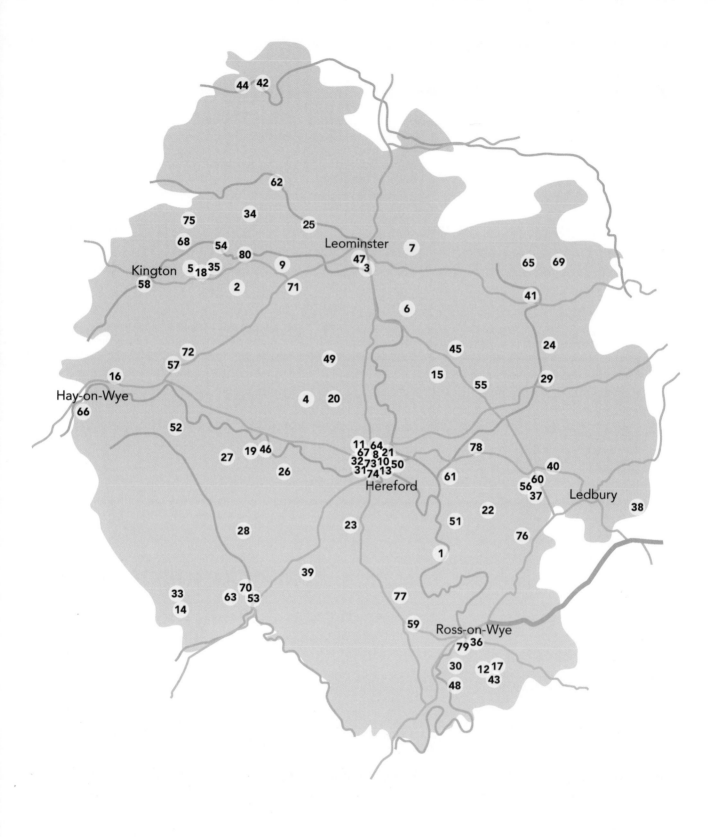

44 42

62

75   34   25

68   54
          80   Leominster   7
5 18 35   9   47
Kington   3   65 69
58   2   71

                              6   41

                      49   45   24

72   15   55   29
57
16   4   20

Hay-on-Wye
66   52

        27 19 46   11 64   78
                              67 8 21
                              32 7310 50   40
                      26   31 74 13   61   56 60
                                  Hereford   37   Ledbury
                                              38
                                              22
                              23   51   76

        28   1

        39

33   70   77
    63 53
14   59   Ross-on-Wye
                                  79 36

                              30   12 17
                              48   43

Location map

Utensils

Contents

Scrumptious starters and inviting appetisers

Mouthwatering mains

Delectable desserts and sweet treats

Cool cocktails and refreshing drinks

Scrumptious starters
and inviting appetisers

Gwatkin Cider

"With a total of 14 local ciders and 8 perries, we are rightly proud of our cider making heritage. In 1992 my Dad and I made a single barrel of perry, just for our own tippling. One day a certain Jon Hallam pulled up in the yard and after we'd given him a glass of perry, he was so impressed that he wouldn't leave until we sold him five gallons. Then the telephone started ringing and now we barrel quite a lot – 10,000 gallons this year. We've also won quite a few awards for our ciders and perries, and we now have an additional string to our bow – the 'Down on the Farm' Festival which we hold every July. Now that's what I call music!" **Dennis Gwatkin**

Serves: **4**

- 500g (1lb 2oz) parsnips, peeled and chopped
- 1 tablespoon olive oil
- 1 teaspoon honey
- 1 knob butter
- 1 large onion, peeled and diced
- 1 large eating apple, peeled and chopped
- 2 garlic cloves, peeled and sliced
- 275ml (½ pint) Gwatkins Kingston Black Cider
- 425ml (¾ pint) vegetable stock
- 1 large sprig fresh thyme
- 50ml (2fl oz) double cream
- Salt and freshly ground pepper

Parsnip and Cider Soup

1 Preheat the oven to 200°C (400°F, Gas Mark 6). Place the cut parsnips into a baking dish, season well with salt and pepper and toss in 1 tablespoon of olive oil and 1 teaspoon of local honey. Add half the cider. Pop into the oven for 15 mins. Add the chopped apple and stir well, pop back into the oven for another 10 mins until they have a little colour.

2 Meanwhile, heat a large heavy bottomed saucepan over a medium heat and add the butter. Soften the onion until translucent. Add the parsnips, apples (and all the juices) and the rest of the cider to the pan, along with the stock. Bring the soup almost to a boil and reduce the heat to medium-low again, add the thyme sprig.

3 Once all the parsnips are soft, after about 10 mins, remove the thyme and purée the soup with an immersion blender or in batches in a blender. Tip – for a smoother soup, pass the soup through a fine mesh sieve. Stir in the cream and more seasoning. Add a splash more stock or water if you feel it is needed. Reheat if necessary.

Serve with a drizzle of cream and garnish with a thyme sprig. Why not try it topped with a crispy bacon garnish for an extra treat!

thyme

Oliver's Cider & Perry

"It is amazing to think that before the 'Truck Act' of 1887, nearly all Herefordshire farms had apple and pear orchards and would have partly paid their workforce in cider and perry. If you made the best cider, you got the best workers. My grandfather made cider on the farm until he decided, with the advance of mechanisation, that it was unsafe. The move away from horse and man power also left less need for refreshment while on the job! Now revitalised, we use vintage cider apples and perry pears – washed, milled, macerated, pressed and fermented, then matured in old oak barrels. Cider has moved with the times and now is not just the drink of landed gentry and country folk. More sophisticated, well blended ciders and perries can be perfect partners with a wide variety of dishes, including of course, our delicious mussels." **Tom Oliver**

Oliver's Mussel Gratin

1 Scrub the mussels carefully; pulling away the beard and discarding any that are open.

2 Cover the base of a large saucepan with olive oil, add the finely chopped onion and apple, cook over a low heat until soft.

3 Increase the heat, add the cider and the mussels, and leave to simmer until the mussel shells open, about 5 mins. Strain and reserve the juices.

4 Discard the empty half shells and arrange the other half shells containing the mussels in eight individual oven proof dishes.

5 Return the mussel juices to the pan and cook over a high heat until reduced by half. Add the butter and when melted pour the reduction over the mussels.

6 Mix the chopped parsley, breadcrumbs and salt; when ready to serve, sprinkle over each mussel and drizzle with olive oil. Set under a pre-heated grill until golden.

Serve at once with a glass of Oliver's Dry Vintage Cider, and some crusty bread.

Serves: 8
- Extra virgin olive oil
- 1 small onion, finely chopped
- 1 small apple, finely chopped
- 1kg (2lbs 3oz) fresh mussels
- 250ml (9fl oz) Oliver's Dry Vintage Herefordshire Cider
- 50g (2oz) butter
- 3 tablespoons chopped parsley
- 80g (3oz) fresh white breadcrumbs
- Salt and freshly ground black pepper

Ballingham Hall Farm

"Ballingham Hall has been a home to our particular branch of the Watkins family for over 120 years. We have lived and farmed here in what we think is possibly one of the most beautiful spots in Herefordshire. Ballingham is a mixed farm of about 1,000 acres with the River Wye running through it. My father and I work together and one of my greatest pleasures is looking after our pedigree Herefords and rare-breed sheep, some of which can be found on the menus at our hotel Castle House – from farm to fork! I am also in charge of ensuring the farm's kitchen garden produces delicious fruit, vegetables and herbs for the hotel's busy kitchen. I must say I very much enjoy the balance of working on the farm during the busy times and then donning a jacket and tie and being part of the team at Castle House." **George Watkins**

Carpaccio of Hereford Beef, Heritage Carrots and Gooseberries

Serves: 4

- 1kg (2lbs 3oz) fillet of beef
- 1 drizzle rapeseed oil
- 150g (5oz) sea salt
- 8 juniper berries, very finely crushed
- 1 tablespoon cracked black pepper
- Leaves of 1 sprig of rosemary, finely chopped
- Leaves of 2 sprigs of thyme, finely chopped
- 1 tablespoon coriander seeds, crushed
- 1 teaspoon grated orange zest
- 1 teaspoon grated lemon zest
- Salt and freshly ground pepper
- 12 heritage carrots (if not available use baby bunched)
- 12 gooseberries
- 50g (2oz) caster sugar
- 1 bunch of watercress

1 Heat a heavy pan until very hot, then sear the fillet in a little oil over a high heat until nicely coloured on all sides. This should take about 3 mins. Remove from the pan.

2 Mix together the sea salt, juniper berries, pepper, rosemary, thyme, coriander seeds and orange and lemon zest on a baking tray, then spread out in a 3mm thick layer. Roll the warm fillet in the spice mixture making sure it is well coated all over. Wrap tightly in cling film and leave to infuse at room temperature for about 2 hours then freeze for about 4 hours until solid to make it easier to slice.

3 Wash the carrots and cut in half, top and tail the gooseberries and slice into 4. Place the sugar into a pan with 2 tablespoons of water and bring to a simmer; allow to cool then pour over the gooseberries.

4 To serve, carefully slice the fillet as thinly as possible, and arrange on a plate. Coat the carrots in a little rapeseed oil to give a nice glaze. Place on the fillet and scatter with gooseberries and finish with some watercress.

Cobrey Farms

"We started farming in Herefordshire's Wye Valley four generations ago in 1925 as tenant farmers of the Guy's Hospital estate. In 2003 the first asparagus was planted on the farm and ten years later Wye Valley Asparagus is famous for its consistently high quality and extended harvest season. Asparagus (a member of the Lily family) is a perennial crop which can produce for about 15 years without being replanted, and consumes less irrigation water than any other UK vegetable. Asparagus is high in folic acid, vitamins A and C, fibre and rutin but contains no fat or cholesterol and is low in salt. What a super food!" **Chris Chinn**

Serves: 8
- 500g (1lb 2oz) strong white flour
- 7g (¼oz) dried yeast
- 1 teaspoon salt
- ½ teaspoon sugar
- 300ml (11fl oz) warm water
- 1 tablespoon olive oil
- 1 bundle, approx. 250g (9oz) British asparagus, cut into 2 inch pieces
- 60g (2½oz) black or green olives, pitted
- 75g (3oz) sun dried tomatoes, halved
- 1 tablespoon olive oil

Asparagus, Sundried Tomato and Olive Focaccia

1 Place the flour in a large wide bowl. Tip in the dried yeast, salt, and sugar, mix and make a well in the middle.

2 Pour the olive oil into the warm water then gradually pour it into the well and mix bit by bit. Use your hand in a claw like shape to combine the mixture. You might not need all the water or you might even need some more, but mix well until a soft dough is formed. Then tip out onto a floured surface and knead for 10 mins.

3 Pop the ball of dough into an oiled bowl, cover, place in a warm location and let the dough rise.

4 Once it has doubled in size, knock it back and then stretch it out to fit a large baking tin. Then let it rest again for a further 15 mins. Meanwhile, preheat your oven to 200°C (400°F, Gas Mark 6).

5 After 15 mins sprinkle over the British asparagus, olives and tomatoes and then press down with your fingers into the dough. Drizzle with the olive oil. Season well and bake for 20 mins until golden.

Serve on a balmy summer's evening with olive oil and balsamic vinegar to dip.

Legges of Bromyard

"As the owner of Legges of Bromyard, I am extremely proud of what we have achieved, I am also very aware that you are only as good as the staff that surround you – I'm pleased to say that mine are some of the best! We have our butchers Arthur, Charles, Andrius and our youngest recruit Tyrone, who all ensure that the meat, sausages and fish on the counters look fantastic. Then we have Ingrid, Sue, Emily, Hollie and Ella in the shop, who are always unphasable and welcoming. Our fantastic pies, ready meals, chutneys and various other seasonal creations are down to the work of our team in the kitchen, Gemma, Danute and Lisa. Not forgetting Ella and Evan who are always on hand during holidays and busy times, as well as Jen, without whom our admin would go to pieces. We all have a passion for great local food and drink and so our shop bustles with customers far and wide." **Anthony Legge**

Legges Rich Liver Pâté

1 Pick over the liver, trimming and discarding any tough membranes or coarse ventricles, and chop roughly. Sweat the onion in the butter until soft and translucent. Warm up the milk with the cream, add the breadcrumbs and leave to soak for 5 mins.

2 Put all the ingredients (except the bacon rashers) into a food processor and pulse for several bursts until thoroughly mixed. Put the mixture into a large or two medium terrine dishes, which can be lined with the stretched rashers of bacon or greased with a little butter.

3 Cover with a lid or double layer of buttered foil. Place in a roasting tin and pour enough boiling water into the tin to come half way up the side of the dish. Put into a moderate oven for 1¼-1¾ hours. The pâté is cooked when it comes away from the side and is firm to the touch. Remove from roasting tin and press with a weighted board or similar while cooling.

Serve on toast, with a dressed salad and chutney (we sprinkled ours with herbs containing dried edible flowers).

Serves: 8-10
- 750g (1lb 10oz) fresh liver
- 1 large onion
- 1 knob of butter
- 150ml (¼ pint) whole milk
- 1 tablespoon double cream
- 100g (3½oz) breadcrumbs
- 250g (9oz) minced pork
- 1 splash of port
- A couple of sage leaves, chopped
- 1 sprig of thyme
- 1 pinch of ground mace
- 1 pinch of cayenne pepper
- ⅓ teaspoon salt
- Streaky bacon rashers to line the dish (optional)
- Freshly ground black pepper

pig

Lower Buckton Country House

"There is an entry in my Visitors' Book describing me as an original 'food terrorist'! My stance against food from multi-national supermarkets is well known. Instead I prefer to support local independent growers, producers, shops and suppliers in Herefordshire. At my off-the-beaten-track country bed and breakfast there's fresh, seasonal food from garden and farmyard throughout the year. I run AGA Cook Days and Food Safaris and am a proud and enthusiastic member of Slow Food, supporting its ethos through a better understanding of food, its taste, quality and production. Oh, and I even co-founded and am a Director of Mortimer Country Food Fair which is held every July!" **Carolyn Chesshire**

Twice-baked Goat's Cheese and Greens Soufflés

1 Preheat the oven to 200°C (400°F, Gas Mark 6). Using a pastry brush, liberally butter four ramekins. Separate the eggs (and set aside). Steam the greens for 3 mins, squeeze out excess moisture, and roughly chop (set aside).

2 Melt the butter (I use Netherend Dairy) in a 2l (4 pint) heavy-bottomed saucepan over a low heat. Add the flour (I use Bacheldre Mill) and form a roux. Cook for a couple of mins until it smells 'biscuity'. Take off the heat, add the milk (I use Bartonsham Farm Dairy) a little at a time, use a balloon whisk and stir well to keep the lumps at bay. When all the milk is added place on a low heat, keep stirring/beating whilst bringing to the boil. Simmer gently for 2-3 mins.

3 Add the greens, sage and goat's cheese (I use Neal's Yard Creamery), stir over a low heat until the cheese is melted. Season with a little salt and pepper to taste. Remove from the heat and beat the egg yolks into the mixture.

4 Whisk the egg whites until they are stiff. Add a spoonful of whites to the cheese sauce and stir in well to loosen the mixture then, using a metal spoon, gently fold in the remaining egg whites.

5 Place the ramekins into a baking tray and divide the mixture between them. Run the point of a knife around the inside edge of each ramekin. Slide the tray into the oven, half-fill with very hot water and bake for about 10 mins or until the soufflés are well-risen, golden-brown and set.

6 Remove the tray from oven, carefully lift out the ramekins (if you don't want to do the twice-baking they can be eaten immediately at this stage) and leave to cool. Don't worry about them sinking. You can leave them in the fridge overnight.

7 When you want to serve them, loosen each soufflé by running a knife around the inside of each ramekin, turn out onto your hand and place them upside down on a baking tray lined with parchment. Combine the breadcrumbs and hard cheese (I use Monkland Dairy) and sprinkle over each soufflé. Pour over the cream and bake in pre-heated hot oven at 220°C (425°F, Gas Mark 7) until they puff up. Serve now!

Serves: 4

- 3 eggs (from the most free-ranging and wildest hens you can find)
- 25g (1oz) butter (make sure it's British)
- 25g (1oz) plain flour (all the better for being traditional stone-ground)
- 150ml (5fl oz) full-cream British milk
- 75g (3oz) local goat's cheese, chopped into small pieces
- 25g (1oz) greens (a handful of spinach or chard from the garden or local farmers' market)
- 1 teaspoon sage, (fresh from your garden or windowsill), finely chopped
- Salt and freshly ground pepper
- 2 tablespoons breadcrumbs
- 2 tablespoons grated hard cheese
- 4 tablespoons double cream

free range egg

JJ Potatoes

"When potato plants bloom, they send up five-lobed flowers that spangle fields like fat purple stars. By some accounts, Marie Antoinette liked the blossoms so much that she put them in her hair. Her husband, Louis XVI, put one in his buttonhole, inspiring a brief vogue in which the French aristocracy swanned around with potato plants on their clothes. The flowers were part of an attempt to persuade French farmers to plant, and French diners to eat this strange new species. Today the potato is the fifth most important crop worldwide, after wheat, corn, rice and sugar cane. Here in Herefordshire potatoes are a mainstay to the farming community and our local economy, providing work and an income for many of our farms, supplying not only many local chip shops (like us) but also nationwide supermarkets. These blinis are great as little canapés, or as starter, or just a great snack." **James Davies**

Potato Blinis

1 Steam or boil the potatoes in their skins, until cooked through. Whilst still warm, peel off the skins and push through a fine sieve.

2 Weigh out 300g of cooked potato purée, whisk the flour into the warm potato then soured cream, and whisking constantly, gradually add in eggs. Season. You must make batter quickly while potatoes are warm, and the batter must be thick enough to almost hold its shape, but creamy and smooth. Each potato is different and may require different amounts of flour and crème fraîche.

3 Cook in a very lightly oiled non stick frying pan on a medium heat. Ladle the mixture into the hot pan. Use 1 teaspoon for canapé or ½ tablespoons for starter.

4 Cook until brown on bottom side, then careful turn and cook until brown on other side, usually ½ minute for each side depending on the size of blinis.

Serve immediately, either simply with local butter, or top with local smoked trout or some home grown tomatoes and fresh herbs. Sometimes with this kind of blini, simple is best.

Makes: 30
- 500g (17½oz) Herefordshire potatoes (we used Sagitta variety)
- 30g (1¼oz) all purpose flour
- 50g (2oz) crème fraîche
- 2 whole eggs (organic)
- 1 egg yolk (organic)
- Salt and freshly ground pepper

Dewsall

"Our Dewsall Court is surely one of the most lovely corners of Herefordshire, with its organic gardens augmented by our longstanding gardener Ruth. There are hosts of wild flowers and butterflies, two different woodpecker species, nuthatches and goldfinches not to mention the annual visitation of swooping swallows and house martins. Beyond the gardens we have bats, hares, deer and large carp that live in the lake, and have lived at Dewsall longer than we have! Sitting under the willow tree on the old oak chairs watching and listening to the goslings, ducklings and baby moorhens scooting across the water is all part of a summer Dewsall afternoon." **Samantha Vaughan**

Beetroot and Goat's Cheese Terrine with Beetroot Consommé

1 For the terrine, cook the beetroots in boiling water until tender – about 30 mins. Peel and let them cool, then slice thinly. Line a bread tin with cling film leaving some overhang to fold over once the terrine is completed. Layer the beetroot slices and goat cheese, seasoning with salt and pepper, dotting with a little zest and a small drizzle of olive oil between layers. Start with the lighter, golden coloured beetroot first, followed by a layer of goat cheese followed by more golden beetroot until they are finished. Then repeat with the red beetroot and goat cheese, ending with a beetroot layer. Finally fold the cling film over to seal the terrine. Place a weighted bread tin on the terrine so it compresses. Pop in the fridge to chill overnight. When you are ready to serve, pull the terrine out of the tin on to a board. Unwrap the terrine and carefully slice with a very sharp knife into 1.5cm (½ inch) slices.

2 For the dressing, blend together all the ingredients in a food processor to give a smooth green emulsion.

3 For the consommé, gently simmer the stock, beetroots, carrots, and onion celery and leeks until the vegetables are soft and the liquid is red, about 1½-2 hours. Strain through a cheesecloth-lined sieve. Do not press the vegetables. Then return the consommé to the pan to reheat, and add the vinegar.

Serve a slice of the terrine, with a flourish of the dressing, and pour the consommé into a small cup on the side, and top with a curl of orange zest.

Serves: 10
For the terrine:
- 12 beetroots (multi-coloured if possible)
- 500g (1lb) soft goat's cheese
- Zest of 1 orange
- Salt and freshly ground pepper
- 1 splash olive oil

For the dressing:
- 1 tablespoon Dijon mustard
- 300ml (10½fl oz) oil
- 100ml (3½fl oz) red wine vinegar
- 2 tablespoons fresh herbs, finely chopped (such as chives, parsley, chervil, lemon balm)
- 1 egg
- 1 pinch of sugar
- Salt and freshly ground pepper

For the consommé
- 1.8kg (4lbs) uncooked beetroots, peeled and chopped
- 3.5l (6 pints) beef stock
- 4 carrots, chopped
- 1 onion, chopped
- 2 sticks celery, chopped
- 2 leeks, chopped
- 4 teaspoons red wine vinegar
- 8 curls of orange zest

The Temple Bar Inn

"The Temple Bar Inn was first licensed in the 1850's, and has also been used over the years as a court house, corn exchange, and stable. Previous innkeepers claim to have seen ghosts of a boy and a dog as well as other apparitions in the oldest parts of the building, and it has been suggested that the land on which it is built has links with the Knights Templars. We have extensively and sympathetically refurbished The Temple Bar Inn, it is now a freehouse (our bar serves several local brews) and the weekly changing menus feature fresh food supplies sourced locally wherever possible." **Philly Jinman**

Smoked Salmon and Crab Roulade with Pickled Veg

1 To make the crab filling, mix the fresh brown crab meat with the rapeseed mayonnaise, chives and lemon juice, then combine with the freshly picked white crab meat. Season with the Maldon sea salt and freshly ground pepper. Set aside.

2 Lay 3 layers of overlapping cling film about 45cm (18 inches) long onto your work surface. Brush lightly with rapeseed oil. Lay the smoked salmon (we used Lay and Robson) onto the cling film in a rectangular shape about 20 x 25cm (10 x 8 inches) and try to make sure there are no holes. Spread the crab mixture onto the salmon leaving a 5cm (2 inch) border all around. Lift up the front edge of the cling film and slowly roll the salmon into a cylinder (like a Swiss roll). Keep the tension of the cling film taut as this will ensure the roulade keeps its shape when cut and served. Secure both ends of the roulade with string, then leave to firm up in the fridge for 2-3 hours.

3 For the pickling liquor, bring the vinegar, chopped chilli, pink peppercorns and sugar to the boil, then set aside to cool slightly.

4 For the vegetables, slice the carrots in half lengthways and cut the radishes in half. Slice the beetroot thinly with a knife (or Japanese mandolin if you have one). Place all the vegetables in a heat proof bowl and pour over the warm pickling liquor. Cover with cling film and leave to cool completely.

5 To assemble the dish, remove salmon roulade from the fridge and trim both ends to remove the string. Cut the roll into 4 equally sized portions and remove the cling film that surrounds them. Drain the liquor from the vegetables and pat dry with kitchen towel. Place each portion to one side of a serving plate, then arrange the vegetables around the roulade. Garnish each plate with a few edible flowers. Drizzle a little rapeseed oil around each plate and finish with a twist of freshly ground pepper.

Serves: 4

For the roulade:
- 400g (14oz) thinly sliced smoked salmon
- 250g (9oz) picked fresh white crab meat
- 60g (2½oz) fresh brown crab meat
- 60g (2½oz) rapeseed oil mayonnaise
- 1 tablespoon chives, chopped
- ½ lemon, juiced
- Maldon sea salt
- Fresh ground white pepper

For the pickled vegetables:
- 250ml (8fl oz) distilled white vinegar
- 1 red chilli, chopped
- 1 teaspoon pink peppercorns
- 3 tablespoons caster sugar
- 8 baby carrot, peeled and cooked
- 1 candy beetroot, peeled and cooked
- 4 breakfast radishes, washed

Edible flowers (to decorate).

Mousetrap Cheese Shops

"Being relative newcomers to rural Herefordshire, we're still in the process of revelling in our freedom from all those humdrum issues that the rest of the county will be only too familiar with. After buying the Mousetrap Cheese shops of Leominster, Hereford (and over the border in Ludlow) in 2012 and moving into the beautiful black and white village of Weobley, it's the little things that continually amaze us. An aeroplane is now an exciting event for the kids rather than a continual drone, the only traffic that we get stuck in is behind a tractor, which you can forgive as you gaze out over the beautiful countryside, and 'spot the barn owl' is a favourite game on the way home at dusk. We must be truly blessed to have found such an established business with a great reputation as the Mousetrap Cheese shops, started over 20 years ago. It's such a fantastic way to spend your day, chatting with lovely visitors and locals who appreciate great cheese and love sampling it with us, along with all the other delicacies that we sell – condiments, crackers and even alcoholic drinks!" **Claire and Matt Knowles**

Goat's Cheese and Lemon Balm Ravioli

1 To make the pasta, tip the flour in a bowl and make a well in the centre. Break the eggs into the well, beat the eggs in the centre, then gradually start incorporating more and more of the flour until all is combined (start with a fork, then switch to your hands). Knead the dough, on a lightly floured surface, really well for about 10 mins until smooth and elastic. Allow to rest in cling film for 30 mins. Then make into sheets with a pasta maker, or with a rolling pin and a bit of effort!

2 To make the filling, combine the goat's cheese, lemon juice and zest, lemon balm and nutmeg then season.

3 Lay two of the pasta sheets on your work surface, then brush both with egg. Spoon 1 teaspoon of the filling at 10cm (4in) intervals along one of the pasta sheets (don't be tempted to overfill or the filling will squeeze out while cooking). Lay the second pasta layer, egg side down on top of the little balls of filling. Gently press together to seal running your finger down between the rows of filling. Using a round cutter, cut circles of the pasta encompassing the filling. Repeat with the other layers of pasta and filling then leave the pasta to dry on kitchen paper for 30 mins or so.

4 For the lemon balm butter, heat the butter in a small pan and once it has started to foam add the lemon balm. Remove from the heat and stir through the lemon juice and zest.

5 Once your pasta has dried slightly, heat a large pan of salted water until boiling, then drop the ravioli into the water. Once they rise to the surface, about 30 seconds cook for another 1-2 mins until cooked through with a slight bite. Serve 3 ravioli per person as a starter or 6 as a main and drizzle with the warm lemon balm butter.

Serves: 4

For the pasta:
- 200g (7oz) Tipo '00' (pasta grade) flour
- 2 eggs

For the filling:
- 150g (5oz) goat's cheese, crumbled
- Juice and zest of ½ lemon
- 6 sprigs of lemon balm, chopped
- ¼ teaspoon grated nutmeg

For the lemon balm butter:
- 3 sprigs lemon balm, finely chopped
- Juice of ½ lemon
- 50g (2oz) unsalted butter

Visit Herefordshire

"Here in Herefordshire, we're far from your average English county. Foodies enthuse about the quality of our produce. Adrenalin seekers rave about our rock faces and river rapids. Then there's the culturally captivated, who take time to live, breathe and absorb our art, history and literature. So, whether your cup of tea is from a thermos flask out amongst our stunning scenery, in a china cup accompanied by a sandwich of the finest Hereford Beef or from a big comforting mug as you dry out from your day's adventure sports, Herefordshire has something for you. Here at Visit Herefordshire, our job is to ensure Herefordshire remains a little bit mysterious but a lot more discovered – and we love sharing something of our lives with you!" **The Visit Herefordshire Team**

Savoury Profiteroles

1 Pre-heat oven to 220°C (425°F, Gas Mark 7). Prepare a baking sheet with baking parchment, a silicone sheet or greaseproof paper which has been dipped in water.

2 Chop the butter into pieces and pop into a small pan with the water, milk, mustard powder, chilli and seasoning. Bring to the boil. As soon as it bubbles, dump in the flour and use a wooden spoon to stir and you have a thick paste. Keep stirring back on the heat for another minute to make sure all the starch has burst – the paste will come cleanly away from the sides of the pan. Put to one side and leave to cool a little.

3 In the meantime, gather fresh herbs and chop. Stir the chopped herbs into the curd cheese and season to taste.

4 Now back to the pastry! In a food mixer, add the beaten egg a little at a time, beating well between each addition until all the egg is amalgamated. Then whizz the mixer up to high speed for a scant minute to create a thick and shiny mixture, then add the grated cheese. Using 2 teaspoons, make approx. 30 rough puffs of mixture, leaving about 3cm between each puff as they will grow when cooking. If you're a dab hand at piping and like a neater look, use a plain nozzle forcing bag to make 3cm puffs. Brush with remaining milk and bake for 20-25 mins. They should be a toasty and shiny brown and pretty hard – this will allow you to fill them without them becoming soggy. Cool on wire racks and at this point you can freeze, or save in an airtight tub for a couple of days. You may need to refresh in a hot oven when you come to use them. Slit the side of the puffs and spoon, or pipe, in the herb flavoured curd.

5 For the dressing, put the cider vinegar, oil, honey and seasoning in a screw top jar and give it a good rattle.

To serve, arrange 3 puffs on a plate with the salad leaves and drizzle over the dressing.

Makes: 30
- 50g (2oz) butter
- 75ml (3fl oz) water
- 75ml (3fl oz) milk
- 100g (3 ¾oz) flour, sieved
- ¼ teaspoon mustard powder
- 1 pinch of chilli powder
- 4 eggs, beaten
- 75g (3oz) hard cheese, grated
- 2 teaspoons milk (for glazing)
- 250g (9oz) curd cheese (Monkland Cheese Dairy Lactic Cheese)
- 2 teaspoons fresh mixed herbs, chopped
- 1 tablespoon cider vinegar
- 1 tablespoon rapeseed oil (Warrens Farm)
- 2 teaspoons honey (Bearwood Bees)
- Salt and freshly ground pepper
- Mixed salad leaves

Mouthwatering
mains

The Riverside Inn

"Herefordshire has truly become the heart of Britain's food and drinks production, with so many high quality ingredients on our doorstep from snails to beef, strawberries to cider it's easy for me to create great dishes, the only difficulty for me is choosing from the vast amounts on offer. Born and raised on a Herefordshire farm with all my family involved in local food, from farmers and gardeners to cider makers and bee keepers, this has given me a knowledge and great love of this region's food and drink. It has shown me the importance of provenance and the benefits of using genuinely local and home-grown produce, seen in our chef-managed extensive gardens. Our 300 year old pub is wonderfully positioned on the southern edge of the Mortimer Forest, right on the banks of the River Lugg. This dish for me sums up the food I love, truly classic flavours that invoke great memories from my childhood. Alongside that, the importance of thriftiness, by using lesser known cuts like cheek and ear give a new interest." **Andy Link**

Cider Braised Pork Cheeks
with Black Pudding and Caramelised Walnut Malted Crumb, Cauliflower Purée and Cider Sauce

1 For the pork cheeks, trim off all outer sinew and bones. Fry the shallots, garlic and celery until lightly brown in rapeseed oil and a knob of butter. Add herbs, cider and brown stock, simmer and reduce by a third. Fry off the pork cheeks on all sides until rich dark brown (this will help to darken and flavour the sauce), add to the sauce. Cook on very gentle simmer for 1½ hours or until very tender, do not disturb too much as it may fall apart. Carefully remove cheeks from stock, cover with foil, keep warm.

2 For the caramelised walnuts, put the walnut halves, sugar and water into a pan, cook on a medium heat to 112°C (234°F) exactly (resembles walnuts in a light caramel). Drain off and deep fry in a pan of oil at 150°C (300°F) until dark brown. Dry on paper.

3 For the black pudding crumb, add the malt extract, black pudding and walnuts into a food processor, pulse into coarse paste, making sure to leave some texture of the walnuts (if using shop brought black pudding, check spice level, adding more seasonings such as salt pepper, ground mace, allspice and cloves if needed).

4 For the purées: Cauliflower – gently cook cauliflower in milk (submerge with extra water if necessary). When soft sieve blend drained cauliflower, adding just enough of the milk mix back to help blend. When smooth gradually blend in butter until glossy, season to taste. Apple – infuse apple juice, cider, allspice and bay, by cooking on medium heat for 10 mins. Leave for 1 hour. Sieve over diced apple rings, add back to pan, very gently cooking for 15 mins. Stand for 30 mins for apple to rehydrate. Add to a blender, slowly pouring in browned butter, until smooth and glossy, season to taste.

5 For the cider sauce, fry off onions and garlic in rapeseed oil. When a light brown, add corn flour, fry off stirring constantly. Add vinegar (the amount will depend on sweetness of the cider used) and some of the reserved cider/pork stock. Reduce by a half or until thick and glossy. Sieve into fresh pan, bring back to simmer, whisk in butter and apple jelly.

6 To finish, place warm cheeks on roasting tin, gently top each with black pudding crumb, ladle a small amount of reserved stock around cheeks, bake at 200°C (400°F, Gas Mark 6) for 15 mins.

To serve, divide the purées on the plates, place the cheeks on top, ladle over the sauce. Add crispy sage leaves (fried in rapeseed oil at 150°C (300°F) until crisp) and Riverside pork scratchings (slow cooked trimmed pigs'ears in court bouillon, coated in polenta, and lightly fried). Enjoy!

Serves: 4

For the pork cheeks:
- 12 pork cheeks (often referred to as plum, as it is a single piece of deep red meat)
- 8 shallots, finely diced
- 4 cloves garlic, finely diced
- 2 sticks of celery, finely diced
- 4 sage leaves
- 4 bay leaves
- 3-4 sprigs thyme
- 1.15 litre (2 pints) traditional, full flavoured local cider
- 1.7 litre (3 pints) brown chicken stock

For the caramelised walnuts:
- 100g (3½oz) walnut halves
- 250g (9oz) sugar
- 250ml (9fl oz) water

For the black pudding crumb:
- 6 tablespoon malt extract
- 200g (7oz) black pudding
- 200g (7oz) caramelised walnuts

For the cauliflower purée:
- 400ml (14fl oz) milk
- 300g (10½oz) cauliflower, chopped
- 50g (2oz) butter

For the apple purée:
- 100g (3½oz) dehydrated apple rings, diced
- 200ml (7oz) local apple juice
- 100ml (3½fl oz) cider
- 5 allspice
- 1 bay leaf
- 30g (1¼oz) butter (fry until light brown)

For the cider sauce:
- 2 onions, finely diced
- 4 cloves garlic, finely diced
- 1 teaspoon cornflour
- 75ml (3fl oz) cider vinegar
- 1 litre (1¾ pints) reserved cider/pork cheek cooking liquor
- 2 tablespoons apple jelly
- 2 tablespoons butter

Neil Powell, Master Butchers

"I started our traditional butchers in 1971 and have maintained all the core values of butchery and many traditional methods. I believe in long-standing relationships with local farms, top quality service and produce. We keep all the processes in-house, from dry ageing the grass fed Herefordshire beef, salting and curing local Gloucester Old Spot bacon, to making our own pastry for our award winning pies. My father was originally based at Longtown and at the core of his business was the 'meat round' where the shop would be taken to his customers and meat would be cut and delivered to the doorstep. My father taught me all I know, and in turn I am passing this onto my sons Peter and Ben. Long may we continue!" **Neil Powell**

Rib Eye Steak, Triple Cooked Chips and Béarnaise Sauce

1 Triple cooked chips take some work, but your efforts will be well rewarded! First, wash the starch from your chipped potatoes under running water. Add the potatoes to a large saucepan of cold water. Heat the pan over a medium heat, simmer until almost falling apart, approx. 20 mins or so. Remove and pop onto a wire rack. Once they have cooled and stopped steaming, place the rack into the freezer for an hour or so. Heat the grapeseed oil in a deep-fat fryer (or a deep pan, not over half filled) to 130°C (250°F). Fry the chips in batches until a light crust forms, approx. 5 mins, remove and drain on kitchen paper. Put the potatoes back onto the rack and into the freezer again for an hour. Heat the oil again, to 180°C (350°F) and fry the chips until golden, approx. 7 mins. Drain and sprinkle with salt.

2 For the sauce, melt the butter over a low heat. As the solids rise as foam, skim this off and continue until there's no more foam, set aside. In a small pan, heat the vinegar, the shallot, peppercorns and 2 tarragon sprigs. Simmer gently until the liquid has reduced by three quarters. Cool the pan slightly then whisk in the egg yolks. Pop the pan back onto a very low heat and keep whisking until the yolks thicken and turn pale, approx. 3 mins. Remove the pan from the heat and add the butter in a thin stream, whisking continuously until you have a thick sauce. Pass through a sieve, and then stir in a squeeze of lemon, seasoning and the rest of the tarragon, finely chopped.

3 Steak needs to rest at room temp before cooking, so make sure you remove it from the fridge about 1 hour before you want to cook it. Preheat your oven to 230°C (450°F, Gas Mark 8). Sprinkle both sides with sea salt, and rub over a little rapeseed oil (we used Brockmanton Rapeseed Oil). Get your griddle pan hot, place the steaks into the dry pan. Cook for 30 seconds (until marked nicely) and then flip. Cook for another 30 seconds, then pop the pan into the oven. Flip the steak again and cook for another 2 mins in the oven (for medium-rare steak, simply add a minute or two for medium). Remove from the pan, cover loosely with foil and rest.

Serves: **4**

For the chips:
- 1kg (2lbs 3oz) Maris Piper potatoes, peeled and cut into chips
- 500ml (17½fl oz) grapeseed (or groundnut) oil
- Salt

For the béarnaise sauce:
- 125g (4½oz) unsalted butter
- 2 tablespoons cider vinegar
- 1 shallot, finely chopped
- 4 peppercorns
- 4 tarragon sprigs
- 2 egg yolks
- 1 squeeze of lemon

- 4 good sized, 21 day dry aged, rib eye steaks
- 1 drizzle of rapeseed oil
- Sea salt

We serve ours with a simple salad and roasted cherry tomatoes.

hereford cow

Westons Cider

"From small pips do apples grow. Westons cider was formed in 1880 by livestock farmer, Henry Weston, as a method of paying his farm workers. As great grand daughter of Henry I am still driving the business forward through changing times and markets. Now over 50 million pints of cider are lovingly produced in this fertile corner of Herefordshire – some still to the original recipes created by Henry. Apples from our own orchards, and from 250 local farmers, are pressed and squeezed, stored and matured. The flavour builds over 6 months and finally the golden liquid is placed in the iconic old oak vats to ferment before our master cider-maker works his magic. Over 30 varieties of cider and perry are produced at the Westons Cider mill, making it one of the biggest producers of traditional cider in the world. If you come to our farm you can even see behind the scenes!" **Helen Thomas**

Rabbit with Cider, Petit Pois and Pak Choi

1 Preheat the oven to 190°C (375°F, Gas Mark 5). Heat a large knob of butter in the base of a large lidded ovenproof casserole dish.

2 Season the rabbit with salt and fry in the butter until browned, adding more butter if needed.

3 Add 2 tablespoons water to the casserole dish. Add the olive oil, shallots, garlic, carrots, celery and bacon and stir fry quickly for a few mins.

4 Strip the thyme leaves and add to the dish with the bay leaves. Fry over a low heat for around 20 mins, pouring in enough cider to cover.

5 Add the peas and cover with lid. Place the casserole dish in the oven and cook for an hour.

6 Remove, stir in mustard and cider vinegar. Add more cider to cover if needed and return to the oven for another hour.

7 Remove from oven, remove lid and place back on hob. Add the pak choi and another large knob of butter. As soon as it has wilted, remove from heat and serve.

Enjoy with a glass of chilled Old Rosie.

Serves: 4
- 2 rabbits, jointed into 4-6 pieces
- 2 large knobs of butter
- 3 shallots, finely chopped
- 2 garlic cloves, finely chopped
- 4 carrots, chopped
- 2 celery sticks, chopped
- 450g (1lb) smoked bacon, chopped
- 1 tablespoon olive oil
- 2 bay leaves
- 3 sprigs of fresh thyme
- 660ml (24fl oz) Westons Old Rosie Cider
- 400g (14oz) frozen petit pois
- 1 tablespoon wholegrain mustard
- 50ml (2fl oz) cider vinegar
- 2 pak choi
- Salt and freshly ground pepper

John Lewis Fine Foods

"We pride ourselves on quick delivery of food and drink to many types of companies, shops and individuals. The produce that we sell and the companies that we provide all have plenty in common, but primarily they all love Herefordshire, seasonal and fresh foods. From our base in Ross-on-Wye we can easily deliver to a broad area – and we are also lucky to have easy access to marvellous local scenery. In the Victorian times Ross-on-Wye was part of the 'Wye Tour' a less expensive and less time consuming alternative to the 'Grand Tour' allowing the middle classes to escape from the dirty, industrial cities to the clean air of the Wye Valley and feel they had had a similar experience. And if you come here today, you will still find the same tranquil beauty of yesteryear!" **John Lewis**

Rotolo of Courgettes, Roast Pepper, Aubergine, Basil and Parmesan

1 To make the pasta, put the flour and eggs in a food processor and mix until they have come together to make a ball of dough (or pasta dough is easy to make by hand too!), turn out onto a lightly floured surface and knead until a smooth silky elastic dough is formed. Wrap in cling film and set aside to rest (and have a rest yourself after the kneading… or maybe treat yourself a glass of delicious local wine) for at least 30 mins. Once rested, split the dough into two (one half of the dough can be frozen at this stage if you don't want to make two). Roll out the dough using a pasta machine, cut into three equal pieces for each rotolo.

2 To make the filling, pan fry or chargrill the aubergine and courgette for approx. 1 minute each side, set aside.

3 Place a sheet of greaseproof paper on a table, place one piece of pasta at the far side of the paper and brush the longest edge nearest you with a little water. Place a second piece of pasta over the bottom edge of the first piece of pasta, repeat with a third sheet so that you end up with one large sheet of pasta.

4 Leaving the long edge furthest from you free of sauce and vegetables to a depth of 2cm, cover the sheet of pasta with a thin layer of tomato paste (or passata). Lay alternate rows of courgette, aubergine and red pepper until the whole sheet is covered and scatter over the basil leaves and grated parmesan. Brush the clear edge with a little water.

5 Now taking the long edge nearest you roll the sheet up as you would a swiss roll, use the paper to tip the rotolo forwards. Take care not to roll the paper into the rotolo. Wrap the rotolo up in the greaseproof paper and lift the it onto a tea towel, tie securely at intervals with kitchen string.

6 Repeat the process with the other batch of dough, and then cook for 30 mins in a fish kettle (or in a deep roasting pan), with enough boiling water to submerge the rotolo.

We served our rotolo sliced, and placed onto of wilted spinach. Finished with a roast pepper sauce (some of the roasted peppers, blitzed, sieved and seasoned), a sprig of basil and a sprinkle of parmesan.

Serves: 4-6
For the pasta dough:
• 400g (14oz) 00 pasta flour
• 4 whole eggs
• 1 good pinch of salt

For the filling:
• 2 large aubergines, thinly sliced lengthwise
• 2 large courgettes, thinly sliced lengthwise
• 2 whole roast peppers, quartered
• 100g (3½oz) tomato paste (or passata)
• 3 sprigs of fresh basil leaves
• 50g (2oz) fresh parmesan

James Moss at The Lakeside

"When we moved from the Black Lion in Hertfordshire to the Red Lion in Herefordshire I thought it was a mad move and that I would find the slow country life somewhat dull. But the metropolis had encroached into our area of Hertfordshire, there were motorways all around us and everything had become about convenience. It is a far cry from the peaceful Shobdon holiday home park – where we are now based at The Lakeside Bar and Restaurant. The holidaymakers are often keen fishermen – trout used to make this recipe was caught locally by Kevin Averill – they often bring back their catch and I cook it for their tea. Much of the produce I use in our kitchens is local, whether meat, veg or fruit. I try to stick to seasonal products – it always tastes best. And as for dull, there's never a dull moment running a business like ours, but the pace and peace certainly suits me better than the relative cacophony of the home counties!"
James Moss

Grilled Trout and Condi Verdi Vegetables with Beetroot and Five Spice Chutney

Serves: **4**
- 4 large fillets of trout
- 1 knob butter

For the chutney:
- 1 tin chopped tomatoes
- 1 beetroot, cooked
- 1 teaspoon of five spice
- 1 onion
- 200ml (7fl oz) malt vinegar
- 200g (7oz) brown sugar

For the condi verdi vegetables:
- 150ml (¼ pint) rapeseed oil
- 1 clove garlic, chopped
- 1 fennel,
- 1 large carrot,
- 1 red pepper,
- 1 courgette
- 1 red onion
- Salt and freshly ground pepper

1 For the chutney, chop the onion and beetroot, add to the tomatoes in a pan. Mix in the five spice, add the vinegar and the sugar cook for 20 mins stirring occasionally.

2 For the condi verdi vegetables, cut all the vegetables into thin strips, keeping them all separate. Warm the oil in a pan with the garlic and 1 teaspoon of salt and a pinch of pepper. Add the fennel and carrot and stir for a minute, then add the peppers and onion and stir, finally add the courgettes and take of off the heat.

3 Score the skin of the fish with a sharp knife and season with salt and pepper. Place the butter on a baking tray and melt under a grill. When melted, butter the fish skin side first and then turn it over so the flesh is on the tray. Grill for 4-5 mins.

To serve, spoon some of the condi verdi into a bowl, place the fish on top. Dot small spoonfuls of the chutney around the outside, and garnish with a wedge of lemon and a fennel frond.

The Handmade Scotch Egg Company

"Our journey has been a bit of a roller coaster ride, eventful, often stressful but always exciting. The enthusiasm and sheer joy the humble Scotch egg can conjure up is truly inspiring. We started our adventure, in 2003, at local farmers' markets popping over the borders to Wales, Gloucestershire and when possible further afield, proudly introducing our innovative Scotch eggs to everyone we met along the way. Originally cooking from home, we now supply independent stores all over the country from our purpose built kitchens in Bishops Frome. Everything is made by hand – cooking no more than six eggs at a time, we think that these are simply the best Scotch eggs around!" **The Eggshed Scotcheggers**

The Herefordshire 'App'
(Apple Pickers Picnic)

1 For the apple relish, peel, core and chop the apples into 5mm (¼ inch) dice. Melt the butter in a saucepan on a medium heat. When it has melted and begins to foam, add the apples and cook for 2-3 mins or until the apples turn slightly golden on the edges. Add the remaining ingredients, stir thoroughly and cook over a low-medium heat for 10-20 mins until reduced and jam-like, the apples should be cooked through but not mushy. Allow to cool before serving, or store in a sterilised jar.

2 Now for the Scotch eggs! Hard boil 6 large eggs (10-12 mins for large hens eggs), cool, then peel. Now roll up your sleeves and get stuck in. Divide your 'scotch' (sausagemeat) into 6 roughly even sized lumps. Flatten each lump between your palms to form 10-12mm (½ inch) thick patties and mould around a peeled hard boiled egg. Place your sausage encased eggs on a breadcrumb dusted tray to prevent sticking. Get two bowls, in one break four or five eggs and whisk briefly. Put the breadcrumbs into the other bowl. Dip your creations in the whisked egg, then toss in the breadcrumbs, and return to the breadcrumb dusted tray.

3 Deep fry at 160°C (320°F) for 7-8 mins (depending on size) shaking/wobbling the cooking basket gently to prevent them from sticking and ensuring an even browned coat. Drain on kitchen paper.

4 Leave to cool for a while to settle and to complete the cooking process. Eat immediately or to save for later allow to cool, cover and then refrigerate (refrigerate within 90 mins and eat within 5 days).

Take them popped in a box to keep them from being squashed. Leave whole for hungry people or cut up to share! No plates! No washing up! Just a few napkins. Enjoy!

Serves: 6

For the Herefordshire apple relish:
- 25g (1oz) butter
- 1 large cooking apple such as the Herefordshire 'Tillington Court'
- 1 large sweeter eating apple such as the Pippin
- 50g (2oz) caster sugar
- 25ml (1fl oz) cider vinegar
- 50ml (2fl oz) cider
- 1 pinch of salt

For the traditional handmade Scotch eggs:
- 10 large free-range hens eggs
- 500g (1lb 2oz) pork sausagemeat, preferably coarse cut, free-range
- 500g (1lb 2oz) fresh breadcrumbs, day old bread is ideal and a mixture of varieties gives a great coating
- 2 litres (3½ pints) cooking oil

An alternative to sausage meat is to buy sausages from your local farmers market, butchers or deli, and remove the skins. Tip – running them under a cold tap first will make it easier. Experiment with all the different flavours and varieties available.

Fillet of Hereford Beef, Hampton Bishop Asparagus, Chase Rhubarb Shallots, Celeriac Purée and Confit Potatoes

Serves: 4
- 4 fillets of beef
- 16 fresh asparagus spears
- 300ml (11fl oz) beef jus
- 4 banana shallots
- 1 celeriac
- 12 new potatoes
- 250g (9oz) butter
- 570ml (1 pint) full fat milk
- 50ml (2fl oz) Chase rhubarb liqueur
- 2 sprigs thyme
- 200ml (7fl oz) vegetable stock
- 1 dash of olive oil
- Salt and freshly ground pepper

1 For the shallots, peel and halve the shallots length ways. Place in a saucepan and cover with the vegetable stock and poach for 5 mins, then remove them and place them cut side down into the Chase rhubarb liqueur to marinate.

2 For the confit potatoes, peel the new potatoes with a knife to resemble small barrels. Melt the butter in a small saucepan, add a pinch of salt and a sprig of thyme, then add the potatoes, bring to a low simmer and poach gently until tender, approx. 20 mins. Then remove from the heat.

3 For the celeriac purée, peel and dice the celeriac then place in a saucepan. Cover with the milk and add a pinch of salt. Cook until tender, then drain and purée in a blender with a little of the milk until smooth.

4 Prepare the asparagus and blanch in boiling salted water for 2 mins, then plunge them into iced water and drain.

5 For the fillet, season the fillets and pan fry in a little oil for 4 mins. Remove the shallots from the liqueur and add to the pan, turn the fillet and cook for a further 4 mins. Then remove and leave to rest for 3 mins. Add the rhubarb liqueur to the jus and reduce until it becomes sticky. While the fillet is cooking warm the celeriac purée and reheat the asparagus.

6 To serve, warm 4 plates, place two spoons of celeriac purée on opposite sides of the plate and drag with the back of a spoon in opposite directions. Slice the fillets in half through the middle and place in the centre of the plate, place 3 potatoes along the side and top with the shallots and asparagus and finish with a trickle of jus.

asparagus

Castle House

"In 2006, when my father David Watkins noticed that the Castle House hotel was for sale, he had, what could be termed, a 'Victor Kiam' moment! In the ensuing years he has made many changes and additions and I can proudly say that Castle House has become Herefordshire's favourite boutique city hotel. There are now twenty four luxury guestrooms, eight of which are in Number 25, a Georgian townhouse, just yards away. Our two-rosette restaurant is well-known for its freshly cooked, seasonal menus. Steeped in her Herefordshire roots, our Head Chef Claire Nicholls sources as much produce as she can from around the Marches, including our own Ballingham farm. When not farming at Ballingham, I really enjoy working at the hotel and welcoming guests who come from far and wide for holidays, weddings or business."
George Watkins

Café @ All Saints

"As a passionate foodie it's been stimulating to be able to develop a café in such an awe inspiring space as All Saints. The stunningly re-ordered All Saints Church is a vibrant parish church with regular services of worship and has been a focus of Hereford life for over 800 years! Its dramatic twisted spire reaches up to dominate the Hereford skyline, whilst inside, the church now serves the human need for physical and social (as well as spiritual) nourishment, with an array of dishes using wonderful local produce! Everything at our café is made on site - here we share our famous Herefordshire beefburger recipe; great beefburgers are all about simple perfection. Getting the details right will make the difference between an ordinary burger and a thing of luscious joy!" **Bill Sewell**

The All Saints Herefordshire Beefburger with Homemade Sesame Baps

1 For the homemade sesame baps, mix the flour (we use Dove's Organic), water, olive oil salt and dried yeast together. Knead for 5-10 mins until you have a sticky, but smooth and elastic, dough. Leave to rise in a warm place covered with either clingfilm or a damp cloth for 1-2 hours, until at least doubled in size.

2 Pre-heat the oven to 220°C (425°F, Gas Mark 7). Weigh the dough in to 70g (2½oz) blobs and shape them into fat little discs about 10cm (4 inch) in diameter and put on a floured baking tray. The dough will shrink a little when cooked and the objective is for the burger – which is 9cm (3½ inch) diameter – to come right to the edge of the bun for maximum deliciousness. Brush the tops of the buns with the egg mixture and sprinkle generously with sesame seeds. Leave to prove for about half an hour until they've puffed up significantly and then bake for about 12 mins until just going golden on top. They should sound hollow when tapped on the bottom. Allow to cool on a wire rack.

3 For the burgers, mix the mince (we source ours from Neil Powell) and hard beef fat with the seasoning thoroughly but gently. Weigh the burgers out at 170g (6oz) each (unless you want some smaller ones for children) and then using a 9cm (3½ inch) scone-cutter or similar make shape them into fat little discs about 10cm (4 inch) in diameter. Cook the burgers on a very hot grill or griddle for 3-5 mins on each side. How long you cook them for depends on your personal taste and the heat of your grill. We aim to get them so that the pink is just fading from the meat but it's still thoroughly juicy.

4 While you're cooking the burger split the correct number of buns, butter both halves and spread the bottom halves with onion marmalade. About a minute before the burgers are ready put the buns in a hot oven. When you think the burgers are done put a slice of cheese on each one and put it back in the heat for a few seconds just to let the cheese begin to melt. Then assemble the burgers: Warm bun with onion marmalade on; burger with just-melting cheese on; slice of tomato, sliced gherkin, top of bun. Then join the whole thing together with a burger skewer so it doesn't topple over on the way to the table!

Tip – of all the details, getting great quality minced chuck steak from a butcher you know and trust is the thing which will make the biggest difference.

Serves: 10 (if you're going to do it properly, then it's more worthwhile for a party than for a solo munch in front of the telly)

For the baps:
- 1.5kg (3lbs 5oz) strong white bread flour
- 950ml (33½fl oz) lukewarm water
- 100ml (3½fl oz) extra virgin olive oil
- 25g (1oz) salt
- 2 x 7g (¾oz) packets instant yeast
- 100g (3½oz) sesame seeds
- 2 eggs, lightly whisked

Note: This makes a lot of baps (about 40), but they freeze extremely well and I never want to make tiny quantities of bread at home – too much effort for too little result. These baps are a treat in themselves (I like to split and warm one in the oven with butter and onion marmalade for a snack).

For the burgers:
- 1.6kg (3lbs 8oz) freshly minced well-trimmed chuck steak
- 200g (7oz) hard beef fat minced and mixed in
- 20g (¾oz) salt
- 1 teaspoon freshly ground black pepper

The trimmings:
- 10 homemade sesame baps
- 150g (5oz) onion marmalade
- 10 very thin slices of emmental or other good melting cheese
- 10 slices of good ripe large tomatoes
- 10 sweet-cured gherkins sliced very thinly
- 10 burger skewers

Wild Mushroom Wellington with Cranberry Jam and Calvados Sauce

1 Roll out the pastry into two rectangles, 30 x 23cm (12 x 9 inches). Cover and leave in fridge to chill, making handling later much easier.

2 To make the filling, fry onion with garlic until golden, remove and set aside. Add all the mushroom and the tarragon to the same pan and cook through. Halfway through cooking add the tamari, seasoning and marsala wine. Cook through until the mushrooms have taken on a good colour. Put the onions, and mushroom mixture into blender. Blend until it forms a purée. Add a little more liquid if necessary. This could be water, more marsala wine or the juice from the cooked mushrooms. Add the rest of the ingredients and knead lightly. The mixture should hold its shape. If you have time, chill it until it is firm enough to handle easily. Preheat oven to 220°C (425°F, Gas Mark 7).

3 Now for the assembly… halve the filling and make a sausage shape with each half. Your sausage should be the length of the about 25cm (10 inches) long and 6cm (2½ inches) wide. Place the filling in the middle of the puff pastry. Make diagonal cuts at a 45° angle with a sharp knife all the way down on both sides. The strips need to be about 2cm (¾ inch) wide. Fold the end pieces in first, then draw the strips across each other to make a plait. Wrap it all nice and snuggly. Don't worry about this too much, so long as you are happy with the look it will not make a difference to the taste, I promise you. Repeat the process for the second wellington. Tip – this will freeze fantastically at this stage. Glaze the wellingtons with the beaten egg and bake for 35-40 mins, or until the pastry has risen well and is golden brown.

4 For the cranberry jam, put apple, lemon rind and juice in heavy based saucepan with half of the cranberries. Add 50ml (2fl oz) water and bring slowly to the boil. Simmer until the apple is soft and the sauce has thickened. Add rest of cranberries and cook for further 10 mins. To preserve, put into sterilised jars and seal.

5 For the Calvados sauce, melt butter in heavy based saucepan, add flour and cook for 2 mins. Slowly add milk making sure there are no lumps. Simmer for a couple of mins, make sure the flour has cooked out. Take off the heat, add Calvados and season to taste.

Serve two good slices of the wellington (it will be very crumbly so you will need a sharp knife or better still a bread knife) with a spoonful of the cranberry jam and a drizzle of the hot Calvados sauce, and a dressed salad. Alternatively this makes a wonderful vegetarian alternative to a roast, or is just as good served cold!

Serves: 12-16

For the wellington:
- 500g (1lb 2oz) all butter puff pastry
- 60ml (2½fl oz) sunflower oil
- 675g (1½lbs) onions, finely chopped
- 4 garlic cloves, crushed
- 200g (7oz) chestnut mushrooms
- 250g (9oz) mixed wild mushrooms
- 2 tablespoons fresh tarragon, chopped
- 2 tablespoons marsala wine (optional)
- 2 tablespoons tamari (or soy sauce)
- Salt and freshly ground pepper
- 100g (3½oz) cashew nuts, chopped
- 120g (4¼oz) pistachio nuts, whole
- 175g (6oz) fresh breadcrumbs
- 320g (11oz) ground almonds
- 1 egg, beaten for glazing

For the cranberry jam:
- 500g (1lb 2oz) fresh or frozen cranberries
- 200g (7oz) caster sugar
- Finely grated rind and juice of 1 lemon
- 1 small apple, coarsely grated

For the Calvados sauce:
- 100g (3½oz) butter
- 100g (3½oz) plain flour
- 500ml (17½fl oz) milk
- 3 tablespoons Calvados (or more depending on personal taste)
- Salt and freshly ground pepper

Lodge Farm Kitchen

"Please don't be put off by the length of the ingredients and cooking procedures in my recipe, you would be forgiven for turning the page, but this is a wonderful centre piece for a special occasion and really well worth the effort; 'for if you bake bread with indifference, you bake a bitter bread that feeds but half man's hunger' (Khalil Gibran). Our small family catering business is located on our family farm, where we grow many of our own vegetables and herbs as well as keeping a herd of Herefordshire cattle; and supporting our neighbours in using their produce in the creation of our contemporary farmhouse food – delicious!" **Louisa Stout**

The Outdoor Kitchen

"I fell in love with the outdoor cooking habit while living in the Balkans, but Herefordshire's winding rivers, woods and hills provide an amazing choice of hideaways for outdoor cooking. Tucked in the folds of the Brilley Ridge, there's nothing better than making jam with fruit from our local PYO farm, or local bacon and eggs eaten next to the Wye to tickle the taste buds, or porridge cooked on an open fire on the shingle below Bredwardine Bridge (it tastes much better than at home in the kitchen). There is so much fun to be had with the family gathered together, cooking over an open fire in the Kotlich. Everyone wants to prod the fire and stir the pot!" **Trish MacCurrach**

Spicy Meatball Goulash

1 Light a good fire, then in the Kotlich, add the onion, garlic and bacon for the gravy, and fry gently.

2 Place the breadcrumbs and milk together in a bowl for 15 mins, to soften the breadcrumbs, then squeeze the milk out.

3 Add the squeezed breadcrumbs to a separate bowl and mix in all the other meatball ingredients (apart from the flour), until well combined. Form into small balls (less than squash ball size) and roll in the flour.

4 Add the meatballs carefully to the Kotlich and fry off the balls in the oil, turning them regularly, until they are brown, this will take about 10 mins.

5 Add the remaining gravy ingredients and simmer for 15 mins. Move the meat balls around in the gravy carefully at first, so they don't break up.

Serve on a pile of creamy mashed potatoes with a dollop of sour cream and some fresh herbs. If you want to make it more of a soup just increase the liquid and seasoning and add some thickening.

Serves: 4

For the meatballs:
- 1 thick slice of bread, in breadcrumbs
- 4 tablespoons milk
- 1 onion, finely chopped
- 220g (8oz) minced beef
- 220g (8oz) minced pork
- 1 egg, beaten
- 1 teaspoon mixed herbs
- 1 teaspoon mild curry powder
- ½ teaspoon chilli flakes
- 1 teaspoon salt
- 1 pinch freshly ground pepper
- 1 tablespoon plain flour

For the gravy:
- 400g (14oz) tinned tomatoes
- 3 cloves garlic, finely chopped
- 1 onion, finely chopped
- 3 rashers smoked streaky bacon, diced
- 1 squirt tomato purée
- 2 tablespoons sweet smoked paprika
- Salt and freshly ground pepper
- Stock or water to cover
- 1 splash oil (for frying)

The Stagg Inn at Titley

"Fabulous local produce and hard work are the explanations given for The Stagg Inn's success in being the first pub to be awarded a Michelin star back in 2001. The Stagg is at the meeting point of two drovers' roads, set in gently rolling countryside. It has a small pretty garden where Steve grows herbs, edible flowers and some fruit and vegetables. Inside it is rustic in feel with tables sourced from the antique shops of Leominster, pictures and prints of local interest are dotted about and the ceiling of the small bar is covered in over 200 whisky jugs. As well as local foodstuffs in the kitchen there are ciders, perries, Herefordshire wine and spirits." **Nicola Reynolds**

Duck Breast with Confit of the Leg,
with Peas and Carrots and Cider Fondant Potatoes

1 The day before... Remove the legs and breasts from the duck. Remove first bone from the leg, salt and leave for 12 hours. Brown the carcass in oven and fry off vegetables until coloured, deglaze roasting pan with red wine and reduce. Combine bone and veg in a large pan cover with water, bring to the boil and simmer for 4 hours, then refrigerate. On the day... Dry duck legs and simmer in goose fat for 1½ hours or until tender, leave to cool.

2 For the carrot purée, boil the carrots, water and juice until carrots soft and tender (add more water if needed), drain, keep a third of the cooking liquid then blend to a purée with the carrots, season, (if more sweetness is required add a drop of Wye Valley honey). Set aside.

3 For the peas, sauté spring onions, shallots and garlic in the butter until softened. Add stock, reduce by half, add cream, then season. Add the peas and simmer until tender Aed the lettuce when reheating.

4 For the cider fondant potatoes, slice potatoes into 4cm (1¾ inch) discs and cut into rounds with a 6cm (2¼ inch) cutter. Season on both sides and add to a heavy bottomed pan with the butter, then cover with cider. Simmer until the potatoes are just cooked. Turn up the heat to glaze the bottoms, then carefully remove from pan.

5 Cook the baby carrots as you would normally. Sear seasoned duck breasts in a very hot pan, add the legs to crisp the skin, then roast in the oven at 200°C (400°F, Gas Mark 6) for 10 mins. Rest duck breast for 5 mins then slice.

6 Reheat the potato, purée and peas. Spoon carrot purée on to the plate, sweep across plate with the back of the spoon. Arrange the duck breast and half a duck leg on purée. Spoon on the peas, add the whole baby carrots for additional decoration and bite.

We garnish with a twist of crisp potato, and serve fondant potatoes separately.

Serves: 4
- 1 duck
- Goose fat (enough to cover 2 duck legs)

For the purée:
- 8 carrots peeled and diced
- 300ml (10½fl oz) water
- 300ml (10½fl oz) orange juice
- Wye Valley honey (if required)

For the peas:
- 200g (7oz) fresh peas
- 2 finely chopped cloves of garlic
- 4 finely sliced spring onions
- 4 finely diced shallots
- 500g (1lb 2oz) butter
- 570ml (1 pint) chicken stock
- ¼ iceberg lettuce, finely sliced
- 200ml (7fl oz) cream

For the cider fondant potatoes:
- 4 large maris pipers
- 425ml (¾ pint) Herefordshire cider
- 50g (2oz) butter
- Salt

- 8 whole baby carrots

Tyrrells Potato Crisps

"Here at Tyrrells we not only make delicious crisps but we can make them super quick as well! Back in 2011 we harvested local Herefordshire potatoes from the field behind our farm, sliced, cooked and packed them and then delivered them to our nearest farm shop in under 45 minutes! We are also proud of our roots (pardon the pun!) and potato crisps have been made at Tyrrells Court Farm since 2002, using potato varieties such as 'Lady Rosetta' and 'Lady Claire', leaving the skins on for plenty of curl and crunch!"

Handmade Crispy Coated Fish Finger Sarnies with Tartare Sauce

1 For the tartare sauce, put the egg yolks into the bowl, add the mustard powder, salt and pepper. Mix these together well. Add the rapeseed oil in drop by drop whisking constantly with an electric whisk, once a few drops have been thoroughly combined the mixture will start to thicken, add the teaspoon of cider vinegar and continue whisking.

2 Now pour the rest of the oil in a very thin but steady stream, keeping whisking all the time. Mix in the capers, gherkins, shallot, lemon juice and parsley, and set aside in the fridge until needed.

3 For the fish fingers, heat the oven to 200°C (400°F, Gas Mark 6). Brush a non-stick baking sheet with the oil. Cut the fish into 16 even strips. Make a small hole in the large bag of Tyrrells to allow the air out, and gently roll with a rolling pin to crush the crisps. Tip onto a plate and sprinkle over the lemon zest.

4 Season the flour with the pepper and paprika on another plate, and pour the beaten egg into a shallow dish. Coat the fish strips in the flour, then dip into the egg, then roll them in the crisps. Place on the baking sheet and bake for 20 mins until golden.

5 Assemble the fish fingers into the miniature bread rolls with a good dollop of the tartare sauce.

Serve with Tyrrells Sea Salt and Cider Vinegar crisps.

Serves: 4

For the tartare sauce:
- 275ml (½ pint) local rapeseed oil
- 2 egg yolks
- 1 teaspoon mustard powder
- 1 teaspoon salt
- 1 teaspoon cider vinegar
- 1 pinch freshly ground pepper
- 3 tablespoons capers, chopped
- 3 tablespoons gherkins, chopped
- 1 small shallot, finely chopped
- 1 squeeze lemon juice
- 3 tablespoons fresh parsley, chopped

For the fish fingers:
- 1 large bag Tyrrells Lightly Sea Salted crisps
- 450g (1lb) skinless sustainable white fish (e.g. 1 large cod fillet)
- 1 egg, beaten
- 2 tablespoons plain flour
- Zest of 1 lemon
- 1 splash local rapeseed oil
- ½ teaspoon paprika
- Salt and freshly ground pepper

To serve:
- 8 Miniature bread rolls
- 2 small bags of Tyrrells Sea Salt and Cider Vinegar crisps

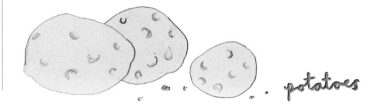

potatoes

Leek, Apple, Sausage and Goat's Cheese Crêpes with Stowe Farm Organic Beetroot Chutney

1 For the chutney, put the chopped onion and vinegar into a large saucepan and bring to a simmer. Add the beetroot, apple, sugar and sea salt and bring the mixture to the boil. Reduce the heat, cover and simmer gently until the chutney starts to thicken. Remove the lid and let the liquid reduce. Pop into sterilised jars and seal.

2 For the filling, heat 1 tablespoon of olive oil in a frying pan over medium heat. Cook the sliced sausage, stirring often with a wooden spoon, until no longer pink. Remove from the pan and drain on paper towel. Pour off the fat from the pan, add 1 tablespoon of the oil, then the apples and a pinch of salt. Cook, stirring often, until the apples are tender and beginning to brown, approx. 4-5 mins. Transfer the apples and sausage to a large bowl. With the last tablespoon of olive oil cook the leeks with ½ teaspoon salt. Cover and stir frequently, until the leeks are very soft, fragrant, and sweet, about 20 mins. Add the leeks to the sausage and apples and gently toss them all together, seasoning as required.

3 For the crêpes, whisk together the flour, eggs, a third of the milk, salt and pepper in a large bowl, until you have a smooth batter. Add the remaining milk and stir well to combine. Melt the butter in a small saucepan, and whisk 1 tablespoon into the batter. Wipe out the pan used for the fillings. Cook the crêpes using the melted butter until golden on each side. Stack on a warm plate keeping warm until ready to use.

4 Preheat oven to 220°C (425°F, Gas Mark 7). Butter the bottom of a 23 x 30cm (9 x 12 inch) baking dish. Lay out the crêpes on a clean work surface. Divide the goat cheese along with the sausage, apple and leek mix equally among the crêpes, spreading it in a thick line across the centre of each one. Roll the crêpes and arrange seam-side down, snuggled together in a single layer in the prepared baking dish. Brush the tops of the crêpes with the remaining melted butter. Bake until heated through, about 10-12 mins, and serve right away.

Serve with a simple salad and a good dollop of the beetroot chutney.

Serves: 4

For the chutney:
- 1.5kg (3lbs 5oz) cooked beetroot, diced into small cubes
- 450g (1lb) Granny Smith apples, finely chopped
- 450g (1lb) onions, finely chopped
- 450g (1lb) granulated sugar
- 600ml (21fl oz) spiced white wine vinegar
- 2 teaspoon sea salt

For the filling:
- 3 tablespoons extra-virgin olive oil
- 225g (8oz) local sausage sliced
- 2 medium tart apples, peeled, cored, and diced
- 4 large leeks, sliced crosswise ¼ inch thick
- Salt and freshly ground pepper
- 110g (4oz) local goat's cheese

For the crêpes:
- 175g (6oz) plain flour
- 3 eggs
- 450ml (¾ pint) milk
- Salt and freshly ground pepper
- 3 tablespoons unsalted butter, melted

... beetroot

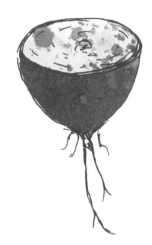

Church Barn Farm Shop

"The Price family have been farming here at Stowe Farm since 1962 and we opened Church Barn Farm Shop in 2011. We all love Herefordshire and the Welsh borders and my enthusiasm for the locality, along with my husband and father-in-law's a deep understanding of agricultural production gives our shop a wonderful ethos. We are passionate about our local producers and very proud of our home made food. My parents are fabulous cooks and using recipes handed down over generations create a huge range of wonderful cakes, pies and meals for the shop. After school the boys and I often sneak round to my mum for a cup of tea with her Victoria Sponge and 'Wish Cakes' (our boys' words for her Welsh Cakes)!" **Ceri Price**

Burton Court

"I have lived at historic Burton Court for over 50 years, which is now a great venue for weddings and corporate events, hosted by my son Edward. However, it is still a wonderful family home. I have alway had a passion for food and food writing. As a Member of the Guild of Food Writers, I enjoy researching and promoting Herefordshire food and have many unique and interesting Herefordshire recipes! My apple and pork recipe stems back to the time when pigs were put to root about in our lovely Herefordshire orchards feeding on wind-fall apples, and when cider sauces were a traditional part of Herefordshire fare. Also, thought to be unique to Herefordshire, local farmers' wives very often cooked a piece of pork alongside their roasting chickens, which helped to baste and add flavour to the chicken." **Helen J. Simpson**

Hereford Piggies in the Grass

1 Split the pork fillets lengthways and open out. Place some cling film on top and beat them flat with a rolling pin.

2 Combine together all the stuffing ingredients. Spread the stuffing evenly over each fillet and roll up and secure then roll them in seasoned flour. Melt the butter in a large frying pan and brown the fillets.

3 Remove the fillets from the pan and add the sliced onion and apples. Fry gently for a few mins and stir in the remaining flour. Add the cider and stock. Bring to the boil. Return the fillets, and simmer gently for 45 mins, or until the meat is tender.

4 Add the cream and bring back to the boil. Check the seasoning. Place on a warmed serving dish and garnish with plenty of chopped chives to represent the grass!

Serves: 6-8
- 2 or 3 pork fillets, approx. 900g (2lbs)
- 25g (1oz) flour, seasoned with salt and pepper
- 75g (3oz) butter
- 1 onion, peeled and sliced
- 2 eating apples, peeled and sliced
- 150ml (¼ pint) Hereford Dry Cider
- 150ml (¼ pint) pork or chicken stock
- 3 tablespoons double cream
- 1 handful chopped chives

For the stuffing:
- 1 lamb's kidney, minced (optional)
- 50g (2oz) cooked ham, minced
- 1 clove garlic, crushed
- 100g (4oz) cooked spinach, chopped
- ¼ grated nutmeg
- 1 tablespoon minced sage
- 1 egg, beaten
- Salt and freshly ground pepper

Brockmanton Rapeseed Oil

"The flowering crop that forms the bright yellow patchwork of our Herefordshire landscape leaves the small black seeds behind that we use to make our vibrant and omega laden rapeseed oil. Did you know that the average UK consumption of vegetable oil per annum is around 50 kilos; and despite recent negativity about crops and bees, our yellow flowers offer a great habitat for thriving colonies. Our own colony of Prices have lived at Brockmanton Hall for three generations, diversifying into different crops and products. Since my grandfather moved here in the 60's we have farmed sheep, dairy cows, arable crops and even trained racehorses." **Ryan Price**

Pan Fried Turbot with Spinach and a Warm Dressed Salad

1 For the dressing, in a medium bowl, whisk together the rapeseed oil and cider vinegar, add a squeeze of lemon, then season with sea salt and black pepper.

2 For the salad, preheat oven to 200°C (400°F, Gas Mark 6). Cut the fennel in half then into 2cm (¾ inch) slices, saving some of the fronds for serving. Coat lightly in the rapeseed oil, place on a baking tray and pop in the oven for 15 mins. Cut the tomatoes in half, and slice the peppers, season with salt and black pepper, and drizzle with a little rapeseed oil. Arrange the tomatoes and peppers on the baking tray with the fennel and bake for a further 15 mins.

3 For the turbot, heat a drizzle of rapeseed oil in a large frying pan over a medium heat. Add the turbot fillets, the thyme and garlic. Fry for 4 mins or until the underside of the fish is golden. Turn the fillet over, add the butter and baste for 2 mins. Remove the fillets from the pan and leave to rest for a few mins.

4 For the salad, bring a pan of water to the boil, blanch the asparagus for 2 mins, then remove and place on a paper towel. Toss the asparagus, fennel, tomatoes and peppers in the dressing.

5 For the spinach, remove the thyme and garlic from the pan, and add a little extra rapeseed oil. Heat the oil then add the spinach. Stir-fry until the leaves have just started to wilt. Season with salt and black pepper, a dash of lemon juice and a little butter.

6 Arrange the spinach in the centre of the plate, place the fish gently on top, and place the warm salad around the outside. Garnish with the fennel fronds and herbs.

Serve and enjoy as a healthy dinner (did you know rapeseed oil is high in Omega 3, 6 and 9!).

Serves: **4**
- 4 fillets of turbot, skinned and boned
- 1 splash Brockmanton Rapeseed oil
- 1 fennel bulb
- 12 cherry tomatoes
- 1 pepper
- 1 bunch of asparagus
- 1 sprig fresh thyme
- 1 clove garlic
- 450g (14oz) spinach
- Sea salt and freshly ground pepper

For the dressing:
- 75ml (3oz) Brockmanton rapeseed oil
- 25ml (1oz) cider vinegar
- 1 squeeze lemon juice

rapeseed flower...

The Colloquy

"I have wonderful old diaries belonging to my great grandmother that chart her life in Herefordshire. Many of the entries revolve around the weather – 'scotch mists', 'raw', 'endless rain' – plus ca change! **'Thursday 17th July 1879: Misty, but no rain! Charlotte left at 11 by trap, much regretted. We drove to Kington with Hilda for the induction of the new Vicar. The bishop gave a most earnest address. Brought Ella back and on arriving home found the new horses had come from Grout of Woodbridge. 'Truefitt and Douglas' are most handsome and rather tired.'** These steeds will have been housed in the original old Victorian stable block which is now our large holiday let, housing not 12 horses, 8 men and 3 carriages but up to 22 holiday guests. Many of the original features remain but I would guarantee that the stable boys were not able to watch Sky Plus TV in a cinema, nor enjoy a hot tub or sauna!" **Jo Hilditch**

Duck and Walnut Salad with Blackcurrants

Serves: 2
- 1 duck breast
- ¼ jar British Blackcurrants in Cassis
- 1 handful strawberries
- ½ cucumber
- 10 walnuts
- 2 handfuls lettuce, lollo rosso and curly endive
- 2 tablespoons olive oil
- Salt and freshly ground pepper

1 Preheat the oven to 200°C (400°F, Gas Mark 6). Cook the duck in the oven for 10 mins, then set aside to cool.

2 Chop the strawberries and cucumber and mix with the salad leaves and walnuts.

3 Mix the olive oil with an equal amount of Cassis from the jar to make a dressing, season to taste. Dress the salad and arrange on a plate. Slice the duck thinly and arrange on top of the salad. Finish by adding the blackcurrants over the top of the salad.

Legges of Bromyard

"I am the fifth generation of a local farming family and have a passion for all things Herefordshire. I am pleased to say that Legges of Bromyard is a bustling shop full of produce sourced with as few food miles as possible. For example all of our meat and game is procured within 6 miles of the shop. My own passion is for pies. The first 'pyes' were made by the early Romans and arrived in England during the 12th century. The word comes from the magpie, our black and white scavenging bird, that collects a variety of items for its nest. We have spent many years perfecting our 'melt in the mouth' hot water crust and encased in the nest a miscellany of different ingredients! A pie is for sharing, as is this recipe." **Anthony Legge**

Legges Game Pie

1 Put the flour, salt and egg into a bowl and roughly mix together. Put the water and lard in a small saucepan and heat together until it reaches boiling point. Stir the hot water and lard into the flour mixture and mix gently until it is combined into a ball.

2 Wrap in cling film and rest at room temperature for 5 mins before moulding into a 23cm (9 inch) pie dish or several individual moulds. It is important to do this while the pastry is still warm, as it will harden as it cools. Make a lid (or lids) by cutting a disc of the remaining pastry to the correct size. Pop a hole in the centre.

3 Once the pastry base is cool, mix the venison, pheasant, rabbit, wild boar, bacon, gherkins and onion in a bowl with the salt, pepper, juniper, mace and nutmeg. Pack the mix firmly into the pastry base, and add the lid.

4 Cover in tin foil and cook at a temperature of 170°C (325°F, Gas Mark 3) for approx. 1 hour.

5 Soften the leaf gelatine in some cold water, and heat the venison stock to boiling point, remove from the heat and stir in the softened gelatine.

6 Gently pour the gelatine through the hole, on top of the meat until the pastry case is full. Decorate with raw cranberries and pour the remaining gelatine over them to hold in place. Leave to cool overnight.

Please enjoy with a glass of chilled Herefordshire apple juice and a fruity chutney (preferably homemade!).

Serves: 4-6

For the hot water crust pastry:
- 225g (8oz) plain flour
- 1 egg, beaten
- 100ml (3½fl oz) water
- 80g (3oz) lard

For the filling:
- 250g (9oz) venison, coarsely chopped
- 250g (9oz) pheasant, coarsely chopped
- 250g (9oz) rabbit, coarsely chopped
- 250g (9oz) wild boar, coarsely chopped
- 250g (9oz) smoked bacon, coarsely chopped
- 125g (4½oz) gherkins, chopped
- 1 onion, chopped
- Salt and freshly ground pepper
- Juniper
- Mace
- Nutmeg

For the topping:
- 200g (7oz) cranberries
- 200ml (7fl oz) venison stock
- 1½ leaf gelatine sheets

Neal's Yard Creamery

"Our Dairy originally made the first Greek-style yoghurt to be sold in the UK, crème fraîche and a couple of fresh cheeses. In 1996 we moved the business from the South East, to our current beautiful location on Dorstone Hill, overlooking the river Wye. We have been able to flourish in Herefordshire, focusing on family and working with a great team to produce the best products we can. Our strong values are at the core of everything we do, both at home and in business, and our small-scale approach to cheese making means that we retain control over every aspect of the production. This even includes our power and heating! As much of our electricity as possible is generated by our on-site windmill (or sourced from ethical suppliers) and our heat requirements are amply handled with our customised furnace, burning locally sourced wood." **Charlie Westhead**

Serves: **4-6**

For the pastry:
- 225g (8oz) plain flour
- A pinch of sea salt
- 150g (5oz) unsalted butter, chilled
- 1 medium egg, separated

For the filling:
- 25g (1oz) unsalted butter
- ½ teaspoon caster sugar
- Sea salt and black pepper
- 600g (1lb 5oz) fresh (shelled) peas
- 2 medium eggs, plus 1 extra yolk
- 300ml (10½oz) Neal's Yard crème fraîche
- 150g (5oz) freshly grated parmesan
- 150g (5oz) Neal's Yard Perroche goat's cheese, cubed
- 1 handful of basil leaves, torn
- 1 tablespoon olive oil

Pea, Perroche and Basil Tart

1 For the pastry, place the flour and salt into a food processor. Dice and add the butter, and reduce to a fine, crumb-like consistency. Incorporate the egg yolk, then, with the motor running, trickle in enough cold water for the dough to cling together in lumps. Transfer to a large bowl and knead into a ball using your hands. Wrap in cling film and chill for at least an hour.

2 To bake the case blind, heat the oven to 190°C (375°F, Gas Mark 5). Knead the pastry until pliable and roll out thinly between 2 sheets of floured baking parchment. Carefully lift into a 23 x 4 cm (9 x 1½ inch) tart tin with a removable base. Reserve trimmings for patching gaps after baking. Prick the base with a fork. Line with foil, tucking it over the top to secure the pastry sides to the tin. Weight it with baking beans, chickpeas or lots of clean copper coins! Bake for 15 mins then remove the foil and patch any gaps or low points in the sides. Brush the case with egg white, then bake for another 10 mins until lightly coloured. This glaze helps to seal the pastry and prevent the filling from soaking into it.

3 For the filling, place 150ml (¼ pint) water in a large saucepan with the butter, sugar, and ½ teaspoon of salt. Bring to the boil over a high heat, add the peas and cook for 5 mins then drain in a sieve. Place half of them in a food processor and whizz briefly to break them up. In a large bowl, whisk the eggs and yolk with the crème fraîche (you can use whipping cream as an alternative), some seasoning and half the parmesan. Fold in all the peas and half the goat's cheese, and add the basil. Transfer the filling to the tart case and scatter over the remaining goat's cheese and parmesan. Drizzle the olive oil over the surface and bake for 35-40 mins until golden and set in the centre.

Leave the tart to cool for 20 minutes before serving. This tart is equally good eaten hot or at room temperature and can also be re-heated.

Weobley Ash

"Our proverbial 'Move to the Country' introduced us to hogs, gimmers, dagging, tupping and more. Yet when it comes to producing tasty, healthy mutton, hogget and lamb, the answer is simple – work with nature. Our experience with lamb is that it is best enjoyed in autumn after a summer on fresh green pasture. As it ages and becomes hogget, the appeal increases as the flavours intensify to a tastier way to enjoy all your favourite lamb recipes. The pinnacle of flavour is found in our mutton, perfect for long slow roasting, rich warming casseroles or simply grilled as a steak." **Helen and David Pickersgill**

Weobley Ash
Moroccan Mutton

1 Roughly break up the half stick of cinnamon and add to a dry frying pan together with the black peppercorns, cumin, coriander and fennel seeds. Toast the spices on a medium heat for around 90 seconds until they start to change colour and give off a scent. Once the spices are toasted grind them to a rough powder either in a pestle and mortar or spice grinder.

2 Place the ground spices into a bowl and add the chilli powder, smoked paprika, salt, and rosemary and mix thoroughly. When the spices are thoroughly mixed add 30ml of olive oil to the spices to create a sticky paste. Finally, add the garlic and mix well.

3 To prepare the meat simply score the surface of the mutton in a diamond pattern, cutting no more than a couple of millimeters into the flesh. Rub half of the spice paste into the meat with the back of a spoon, massaging it in well.

4 Preheat the oven to 230°C (450°F, Gas Mark 8) and roast the joint for 20-30 mins until the cuts open up and the meat has started to brown and sizzle, remove the meat from the oven and spread the rest of the spice mix over the top of the meat with a spoon. Add 300ml (10½fl oz) of water to the roasting tray to get the juices going, and cover the tray with foil. Turn the heat right down to 120°C (250°F, Gas Mark ½) and leave to cook for at least six hours.

5 Once cooked, the meat can be pulled off the bone. It will be too tender to carve so simply pull apart with 2 forks and pour the juices over the meat. We serve ours with couscous and Mediterranean roast vegetables (or why not try in wraps with raw shredded red cabbage and carrot). A family favourite every time. Enjoy!

This recipe will also work well with a shoulder of hogget or lamb.

Serves: 4-6
- 1 shoulder of mutton
- ½ stick cinnamon
- 1 teaspoon black pepper corns
- 1 teaspoon cumin seeds
- 1 teaspoon coriander seeds
- 1 teaspoon fennel seeds
- 1 tablespoon smoked paprika
- 2 teaspoon salt
- 2 tablespoons fresh rosemary, finely chopped
- ¼ teaspoon chilli powder
- 2 tablespoons extra virgin olive oil
- 1 tablespoon of minced garlic

We really enjoy this way of cooking mutton as it can be started in the morning and when you come back at the end of a day outside, the kitchen is full of the wonderful exotic aroma of the cooked mutton, which is tender and falling apart.

The Spiceworks

"Our family business which is based in Hereford is founded on years of experience in the food and catering industry. The world would be a blander place without the enhancement that herbs and spices can bring. Although our company imports herbs, spices, seeds and herbal infusions from all over the world, we are also very proud of our Herefordshire roots. Our Herefordshire grown dried hops are not only for beer brewing, but used alone or in conjunction with other herbs in your pillow can aid peaceful sleeping; our cider apple vinegar is made from local fruits and our dried elderberries are plucked from our local fruit-laden hedgerows. Here we share a great way to spice up one of our favourite Herefordshire crops. East meets West!" **Ed Harris**

Spicy Bombay Herefordshire Potatoes

1 Scrub, peel and cut the potatoes into quarters, then par boil. Drain and set aside.

2 Fry the chopped onions in a little oil until they are soft (a few mins on medium heat – stir all the time to ensure that they do not stick). Add The Spiceworks Spicy Bombay Potato blend and fry gently for 2 mins adding a little more oil if necessary.

3 Add the butter (or margarine) then the potatoes, stir well, ensuring that all the potatoes are well coated by the spices. Cook for 12-16 mins (until the potatoes are soft).

4 Core and dice the tomatoes. Add the tomatoes to the pan, heat through on low heat.

Serve, either on their own, as a quick lunch or snack, with a salad of your choice, or as a side dish to your favourite curry.

Serves: 4-6
- 50g (2oz) The Spiceworks Bombay Potato spice blend
- 4 large potatoes
- 2 large onions, chopped
- 6 tomatoes
- 25g (1oz) butter or margarine
- 1 tablespoon of oil

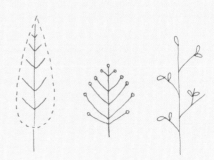

Cargill

"Operating in Herefordshire for over half a century, Cargill's chicken processing facility can process up to 1.3 million chickens a week – that's almost 67 million chickens a year! Started by a group of local farmers in the early 50s the company still has strong relationships with the local farming community so we can trace our supply chain from farm to fork. On a more fun note did you know that the chicken is the closest living relative of the tyrannosaurus-rex; and that the longest recorded distance flown by any chicken was 301.5 feet and was for 13 seconds! Our delicious chicken recipe was created by George Rizzardini, one of our chefs – Italian by name, but Herefordshire through and through!"

Chef George's Chicken Saltimbocca
(Jump in the Mouth)

1 Lay the prosciutto out in 2 sections on a chopping board, divide half the sage leaves and parmesan on to the slices. Place a chicken breast on top. Fold the prosciutto around the chicken to form 2 neat parcels. Season with freshly ground black pepper.

2 In a small non stick frying pan add the olive oil and on a gentle heat sauté the parcels for 10-12 mins turning frequently until cooked. Add the marsala wine and reduce and finish with a knob of butter.

Serve with pasta, green beans and a wedge of lemon.

Serves: 2
- 2 British chicken breasts, approx. 150g (5oz) each
- 4 slices prosciutto
- 6 fresh sage leaves
- 1 tablespoon olive oil
- 25g (1oz) unsalted butter
- 20g (¾oz) parmesan shavings
- 1 small lemon
- 100ml (3½fl oz) marsala wine
- Freshly ground pepper

Rayeesa's Indian Kitchen

"I love the fact that living where we are, we can get great quality fresh produce from local farms, which really makes a difference to the flavours and quality of food. Until I started cooking with game I hadn't realised how well spice works with not only venison, but also pheasant and wild duck. As a spokesperson for the BASC (British Association for Shooting and Conservation) I learn more about all these amazing animals day by day. For example deer live in their established territories for life – it is said that they prefer to go hungry than to leave their territory. When I was young, my mum used to comment about taking home one of the deer in Richmond Park – only now do I begin to understand why!" **Rayeesa Asghar-Sandys**

Rayeesa's Venison Rogan Josh

1 Fry onions until golden brown. Add the whole spices until they release a lovely aroma.

2 Add the rest of the spices along with the garlic and ginger paste, and stir well.

3 When the oil starts to separate add the meat and seal with the spice mixture. Then add the tomatoes and some water and let the mixture cook on a low heat.

4 When the venison is almost tender add the peppers and stir together, let it all cook for a further 5-10 mins. Season to taste.

Garnish with fresh coriander and serve with basmati rice or chapattis.

Serves: 4-6
- 1kg (2lbs 3oz) of shoulder of venison, cut into 5cm (2 inch) cubes
- 2-3 medium onions, sliced
- 1 tablespoon garlic and ginger paste
- 1 teaspoon turmeric
- ½-1 teaspoon chilli powder
- 1 teaspoon paprika
- 2 teaspoons ground coriander
- 3-4 cardamom
- 2.5-5cm (1-2 inch) piece of cinnamon
- ½ teaspoon peppercorns
- 2-3 bay leaves
- 3-6 tomatoes, quartered
- 1 each of red, green and yellow peppers, cut into wedges (optional)
- 1 handful of fresh chopped coriander
- Salt to taste

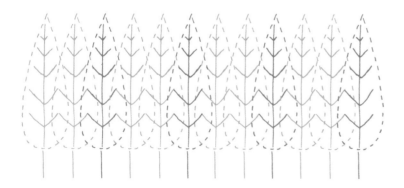

The Mill Race

"At The Mill Race we scour Herefordshire for the best quality ingredients we can find. Our passionate Head Chef, Richard, goes foraging on our lovely Bishopswood Estate in search of wild garlic, watercress from the lakes and other tasty morsels. If we are very lucky he can sometimes be persuaded to shoot us a rabbit or two! Rosie, our very loyal housekeeper, who has been with us since day one, can often be heard bartering with her neighbours for plums and apples! Even our customers are sometimes roped into helping us hunt and gather – they are normally happy to help in return for a pint or two! Using one of the underused cuts, this lamb combined with the sweet tomatoes and the punchy chorizo is a real warmer."
Luke Freeman

Lamb Brisket

1 Mix all the stuffing ingredients together in a food processor until a coarse paste has formed.

2 Lay one piece of breast skin side down, smear with the tomato and chorizo paste, place the second piece of breast on top, skin side up. Repeat until all four pieces of breast are used.

3 Tie the joint together and roast in a low oven 100°C (212°F, Gas Mark ¼) for 4 hours.

4 Take out of oven and when cool enough to handle snip off the strings and wrap in cling film very tightly and chill overnight.

5 To finish slice off a portion and pan roast until browned on all sides.

Serve with a two bone rack of Herefordshire lamb, pea purée made from fresh peas, mint and a little cream, Anna Potatoes (layers of potato and butter cooked slowly until soft) and some Wye Valley Asparagus.

Serves: 6-8
- 4 breasts of lamb, approx. 2kg (4lbs 6oz)

For the stuffing:
- 200g (7oz) diced chorizo
- 110g (4oz) sunblushed tomatoes
- 1 egg
- 1 sprig thyme
- 1 ciabatta

lamb

Roasted Fillet of Herefordshire Beef, Oxtail Hash Croquettes, Stewed Prunes and Ledbury Dark Gravy

1 For the hash croquettes, melt the lard in a large pan, cover the oxtail in half the flour and brown. Add onion and garlic to pan, cook until soft. Add remaining flour and cook for 4 mins, stirring constantly. Slowly add apple juice, beef stock and Ledbury Dark ale. Add prunes and season. Cook for 3 hours in a fan oven set to 170°C (325°F, Gas Mark 3). Allow to cool, remove the meat from the bone and roughly chop with the prunes. Mix with the cooked mashed potatoes and shredded cabbage and shape into 4 croquettes of equal size. Place in fridge and allow to chill for 30 mins. Take 3 small bowls. In the first half fill with plain flour; in the second beat two eggs and the third half fill with bread crumbs. Place each croquette into the flour, then the egg and then cover generously with bread crumbs.

2 For the fillet, take meat out of the fridge 30 mins before cooking. Preheat the oven to 180°C (350°F, Gas Mark 4). Put a tablespoon of oil in a hot heavy based frying pan, season the fillet with salt and pepper and brown the fillet all over. Place on a wire rack on a tray and cook in the preheated oven (20-25 mins for medium 40 mins for well done). Remove and allow to rest for 20 mins.

3 For the celeriac purée, melt the butter in a moderately heated pan (don't burn the butter!). Add the chopped bacon and sauté for 3 mins, until it becomes darker in colour. Add the diced celeriac and a pinch of salt and ground pepper. Stir for 3-4 mins then cover with a lid and cook on a low heat for 10-12 mins until the celeriac is cooked. Add the cream, stir and blitz – it should be perfectly smooth and the texture should resemble thick yoghurt.

4 For stewed prunes and Ledbury Dark gravy, pass oxtail cooking liquor through a fine sieve into a pan, add prunes and bring to boil. Remove prunes and reserve them in a cling-filmed bowl, whilst you reduce the liquid by half. Season and thicken the gravy if needed and reserve until ready to plate.

5 On a low heat shallow fry the hash croquettes in a little vegetable oil until evenly golden brown. Wilt the spinach with a little butter, poach 16 small shallots in water seasoned with salt and sugar.

6 On each plate, place the cooked spinach to one side and place the croquette on top, take a spoonful of celeriac purée and smear a blob with the back of the spoon opposite the spinach. Carve the fillet into 8 even slices (discarding the two ends first) and place two medallions on top of the purée. Place the cooked shallots and prunes randomly about the plates, spoon over the rich gravy and finish with a few sprigs of fresh water cress.

Serves: 4
- 600g (1lb 5oz) centre cut fillet of beef
- Salt and freshly ground pepper
- 1 tablespoon oil
- 500g (1lb 2oz) spinach
- 16 small shallots
- A few sprigs of watercress

For the oxtail hash croquettes:
- 1kg (2lbs 3oz) oxtail on the bone
- 25g (1oz) flour
- 50g (2oz) lard
- 2 large onions, chopped
- 1 clove garlic
- 250ml (9fl oz) apple juice
- 150ml (¼ pint) Ledbury Dark
- 100ml (3½fl oz) beef stock
- 50g (2oz) pitted prunes
- 300g (10½oz) cooked mashed potatoes, seasoned
- 100g (3½oz) shredded savoy cabbage, cooked

For the pane (bread crumb coating):
- 100g (3½oz) flour
- 2 eggs
- 300g (10½oz) bread crumbs

For the stewed prunes and Ledbury Dark gravy:
- Reserved oxtail cooking liquor
- 12 pitted prunes
- 1 bay leaf

For the smoked bacon and celeriac purée:
- 1 small celeriac, diced
- 100g (3½oz) smoked streaky bacon
- 25g (1oz) butter
- 200ml (7fl oz) double cream

A couple of pints of delicious Ledbury Dark Ale, to enjoy with your well earned meal.

Ledbury Real Ales

"Herefordshire cattle are an iconic part of the county's heritage. By uniting our award winning Ledbury Dark Ale with some of the best beef in the country the recipe is a perfect combination of local produce. Ledbury Real Ales is ideally located to make use of the highest quality ingredients to create our beers. We are surrounded by some of the best hops in the world which gives our beers their distinctive flavours. We set up our brewery in 2010 and it has expanded very quickly, largely due to the popularity of our range of high quality cask conditioned real ales." **Kate and Ant Stevens**

Pengethley Farm Shop

"This recipe has been handed down the Honey family. My Grandmother Babs Honey, who use to write in the Farmers Weekly in the 1960's, was given this recipe from her Mother-in-law, my Great Grandmother Honey who lived in Trerice, near Newquay in Cornwall. My Great Grandmother brought up 8 children of her own and her husband's 8 brothers and sisters and my Grandmother raised 8 children of her own, therefore, this recipe will feed plenty. My Great Grandmother use to cook the Cornish Under-roast every Saturday for lunch and my Grandmother continued this tradition. Here we have made the recipe with great local produce from our shop… so have aptly renamed it Herefordshire Under-roast! We hope you enjoy it!" **James and Kate Hughes**

Herefordshire Under-roast

1 Grease a lasagne dish and preheat oven to 150°C (300°F, Gas Mark 2). In a heavy based saucepan or casserole dish, heat up the oil.

2 Coat the beef chuck steak and kidney in the plain flour. Add the beef and kidney to a hot pan and brown the meat. Soften the onions and add the beef and kidney back into the pan. Add the beef stock and Worcester Sauce to the pan. Season with salt and pepper and stir well. Add contents of pan to the lasagne dish.

3 Peel the potatoes and slice into 1.5cm (½ inch) thickness (you will need the potatoes to be thick enough for half the slice to be in the gravy and half to be above the gravy). Place on top of the meat in the dish and then brush with melted butter. Place in centre of the oven and cook for 2-2½ hours until meat is tendered and potatoes have browned on the edges.

Serve hot with plenty of vegetables.

a saucepan

Serves: 6
- 900g (2lbs) beef chuck steak, diced
- 225g (8oz) ox kidney, diced
- 450g (1lb) onions, sliced
- 1 rounded tablespoon plain flour
- 570ml (1 pint) beef stock
- ¾ teaspoon Worcester sauce
- Salt and freshly ground pepper
- 900g (2lbs) potatoes
- 1 knob butter, melted
- 1 dash of oil

Venison and Beef Casserole

1 In a frying pan, brown the cubed venison and beef in the oil. Remove with a slotted spoon and set aside. Add the onions, leek, celery, garlic and carrots to the remaining oil and sauté for about 5 mins, then remove from the pan. With the remaining oil (add a little more if you need to) stir in the flour and make a thick paste. Add the beef stock and wine gradually and combine into a thick sauce. Season to taste.

2 Add the venison, beef, vegetables and sauce into a large casserole dish with a lid and bring to the boil. Transfer to the simmering oven (tastes best when cooked in an AGA!), or in a conventional oven at 150°C (300°F, Gas Mark 2) and leave for 2-3 hours. Remove from the oven, and stir in the soaked apricots along with their water. Meanwhile, make the dumplings!

3 For the dumplings, put the flour and herbs into a large bowl, add in the butter and seasoning. Make a well in the middle of the mixture; add the lemon juice and about 3 tablespoons of cold water. Mix to a soft dough and form into a ball. Roll out on a floured board to about 5cm (2 inch) thick, then cut into rounds using a 7.5cm (3 inch) cutter.

4 Take the casserole out of the oven and drop in the dumplings in a circle, glaze with the beaten egg and pop in the roasting oven, or turn your conventional oven up to 220°C (425°F, Gas Mark 7), to bake for a further 45 mins.

Serve with roast potatoes and seasonal vegetables. A truly delicious and nutritious treat; one that Betty is proud of!

Serves: 6-8
- 800g (1lb 12oz) venison, cubed
- 400g (14oz) beef, cubed
- 175g (6oz) dried apricots soaked overnight in ¼ pint water
- 230g (8oz) carrots, scrubbed and chopped
- 2 large onions, finely chopped
- 2 sticks celery, chopped
- 1 large leek, chopped
- 3 large cloves garlic, squashed
- 2-3 tablespoons plain flour
- 3 tablespoons oil
- 1 litre (1¾ pints) beef stock made from beef bones
- 275ml (½ pint) red (or plum) wine
- Salt and freshly ground pepper

For the dumplings:
- 350g (12oz) self-raising flour
- 4 tablespoons mixed herbs
- 200g (7oz) butter, chilled and grated
- Juice of 1 lemon
- Salt and freshly ground pepper
- 1 egg, beaten (to glaze)

Use organic produce whenever possible.

Betty Twyford

"I am passionate about my message: 'those who eat together, stay together' – my parents and grandparents had every meal together at the same table in their long and healthy marriages. We are in the longest and deepest recession since the second world war and during these trying times we all need to 'make do, and mend'. We need to redress the balance of the throwaway society that we are becoming. You can be sensible and stylish in one breath; eating simple and delicious foods altogether at one table is a step in the right direction." **Betty Twyford**

The Crown Inn, Woolhope

"We wanted to create a traditional freehouse that was at the heart of the village. One that forms an essential part of the community, but also attracts people who want to make a journey to see us. In 14 years in the business, 'local' has always been the default setting. When you have Herefordshire as your pantry, it makes cooking fresh, seasonal, simple food an absolute joy." **Matt Slocombe**

Herb Crusted Rack of Lamb, Summer Vegetable Stir Fry and Heritage Tomato Sauce

1 For the herb crust, put the rosemary, thyme leaves, garlic and a crack of salt and pepper in a pestle and bash! Add the mustard and splash of vinegar, bashing on until you get a bright green pulp.

2 For the rack, preheat your oven to 200°C (400°F, Gas Mark 6). Heat a couple of large sauté pans that will take two racks each. Score a criss cross into the fat and season well. Add a glug of oil in each pan and put racks fat side down into pans. Spit and sizzle! After 2 mins turn to do the edges, repeat until they are golden in colour on all edges. Set aside to cool slightly. Cut the tomatoes into chunks. Spread the herb pulp over the browned racks, pressing and squishing into the grooves. Put the racks, herby side up into the oven on a roasting tray and scatter the tomatoes around the lamb. The lamb will take about 12-15 mins for pink/medium rare. Drink some of the cider.

3 For the summer vegetable stir fry, cut the baby carrots in half lengthways, slice the baby courgettes, beet root, baby onions. You are trying to get all the veggies to cook at the same time when you stir fry them! Slice par cooked spuds. Heat a large wok or heavy based pan. Add a glug of oil, add spuds and colour, then add all the veg tossing and stirring as you go! The veggies deserve a splash of cider too. They will steam and really enjoy it. The veg will be ready when its ready, keep checking for the bite that you like. Then put in a warm serving dish. Sprinkle with the mint leaves.

4 The lamb should be done now, set aside to rest. Take the sloppy tomatoes and the pan juices and pass through a sieve into a small pan. Squash all the pulp well in the sieve. Add a splash of balsamic vinegar to the tomato juices, sprinkle of sugar to taste and stir to reduce a little. Using a sharp carving knife slice the racks, following the bones as a guide. Put a nice pile of veggies onto each plate and fan your lamb onto them. Spoon the sauce around.

Enjoy with the remaining cider, feel free to open extra bottles!

Serves: 4
- 4 racks of lamb (4 bone, half French trimmed, Woolhope reared... if available!)
- 16 new potatoes (par cooked)
- Summer vegetables (mangetout, French beans, beetroot, baby courgettes, baby onions, baby carrots...use whatever you have available, the more the merrier!)
- 3 or 4 heritage tomatoes (or 6-8 cherry toms if that's what you can get)
- A couple of glugs of rapeseed oil
- A few mint leaves
- A couple of bottles of quality dry cider
- 1 sprig rosemary
- 1 sprig thyme
- 2 cloves garlic
- 1 teaspoon Dijon mustard
- Salt and freshly ground pepper
- 1 teaspoon white wine vinegar
- 1 teaspoon balsamic vinegar
- ½ teaspoon sugar

tomato

Monkhide Wines & Liqueurs

"Here in our small, family-run winery in rural Herefordshire we produce a delicious range of Award Winning Fruit Wines and liqueurs. We have perfected our recipes for over the past fourteen years, from a humble beginning of being obsessive home-made wine makers. Our passion and commitment to producing a high quality drink is captured in every bottle. We firmly believe that to have one of the best products on the market we have to invest in using high quality ingredients. We do not take short cuts or use cost cutting methods. Our range is quite varied and regularly includes limited edition wines. If we find a good crop of something we are always keen to get it bubbling away in our winery as soon after harvesting as possible. Every part of the production is done in our winery which means products are of a consistent high quality. Of course, another bonus of being Monkhide is that we love meeting our customers at events and seeing their reactions when they taste our wines and liqueurs." **Anthony and Lorraine Digweed**

Monkhide Apple Brandied Chicken and Pork Brochettes

1 Put the wooden skewers into a bowl of water to soak. Add the lemon juice, garlic, Monkhide Apple Brandy liqueur and thyme into a small saucepan and bring to the boil. Simmer over a lower heat for 10 mins until a nice syrupy consistency.

2 Quickly stir in mustard and honey and whisk until smooth. Take off the heat and put aside to cool.

3 Place the cubed chicken or pork into a bowl, and season well with salt and freshly ground pepper. Pour over the cooled sauce and toss to make sure it is well coated.

4 Thread the meat cubes onto the wooden skewers, alternating with the coloured peppers, and cook on the BBQ or under the grill (medium heat). They should be slightly browned and cooked though after about 10 mins.

Serve with fresh, seasonal salads for a tasty BBQ treat, or on top of a plate of freshly cooked wild rice for a light supper. For a vegetarian alternative, simply use cubes of tofu or quorn in place of the chicken and pork.

Serves: 8-10
- 900g (2lbs) of cubed chicken and (or) pork
- 3 garlic cloves, pressed
- 2 tablespoons freshly squeezed lemon
- 160ml (6fl oz) Monkhide Apple Brandy Liqueur
- Pinch of fresh thyme leaves
- 1 tablespoon English mustard
- 2 tablespoons honey
- 3 coloured peppers, sliced and cubed
- Salt and freshly ground pepper

... a glass of apple brandy

Saxtys

"Our family history in the licensed trade can be traced back nearly 300 years – our family were the original Symonds Cider and English wine company, Herefordshire born and bred. Selling cider wines and spirits (amongst other things) is in our bloodstream and what we do best, and even better if it is locally sourced and produced. At our restaurant all dishes are freshly made on site and cooked to order with an emphasis on using local, fresh ingredients. You can also have a few local drinks, or come for our local DJ's playing funky grooves on Friday and Saturday nights!" **Edward Symonds**

Gourmet Pork and Black Pudding Burger with Herefordshire Apple Chutney

1 For the chutney, gently cook the apples, onions and vinegar for 30 mins. Add the rest of the ingredients and simmer for 2 hours. Finish with chopped mint to taste.

2 The black pudding is made by A.H. Griffiths (a family butchers on the North Herefordshire border – one of the last remaining abattoirs left in this country with its own butcher's shop attached) using a traditional family recipe that has been passed down through family generations. The mix for the black pudding has been perfected over the years, using produce which has come through the abattoir and fine subtle seasoning. The pork burgers have been created by G and R Tudge on their small family run farm in North Herefordshire using superb shoulder meat from their Free Range Rare Breed Berkshire pigs. The pigs are an old slow growing breed which have slightly more fat on than commercial pigs but used correctly provide succulence and flavour! We mix the crumbled black pudding into the burger meat, with a sprinkle of seasoning, caramelised onions and drop of water for consistency… all that's needed to provide a flavour packed, juicy burger.

3 Core and slice the apple into 1cm discs. Caramelise the apple in the butter and sugar. Crisp the oak smoked free range Rare Breed Berkshire bacon and grill the burgers. Stack the burger, bacon and caramelised apple and finish in the oven, for a few minutes. Pop the topped burger into in a toasted brioche bun, stacked on top of the salad.

Serve with plenty of the chutney and home fries.

Serves: **4**

For the chutney:
- 10 Herefordshire Apples
- 100ml (3½fl oz) cider vinegar
- 200g (7oz) sugar
- 500ml (17½fl oz) apple juice
- 2 onions, diced
- 4 pears, peeled cored and chopped
- A couple of sprigs of mint

For the burger:
- 375g (13oz) gourmet Rare Breed Berkshire pork (from Herefordshire raised pigs!)
- 75g (3oz) black pudding, crumbled
- 1 Herefordshire apple
- 1 tablespoon sugar
- 1 knob of butter
- 4 large rashers of oak smoked free range Rare Breed Berkshire bacon
- 1 tomato, sliced
- ½ onion, sliced
- 12 slices of cucumber
- 1 handful salad leaves

Brinsop Court Estate

"Brinsop Court Estate is 800 acres of farmland and ancient woodland. Our guests have the freedom of the estate to roam around. They choose from bird watching to playing tennis, relaxing in the hot tub to walking along our marked trails, fishing in the medieval pools and moat or exploring with Daub and Wattle the ponies, there is something for everyone. With log fires in the sitting rooms and Agas in the kitchens and a stunning banqueting hall and library for special occasions, we can comfortably accommodate from 2 to 28 guests. John Thornley OBE, Brinsop Court Estate's deer stalker, ensures that our resident herds of deer are managed effectively – this is one of his favourite venison recipes." **Pat Churchward**

John's Venison Stroganoff

1 Trim the meat and cut into thin strips. Peel the onions, cut in half then slice into half moon shapes. Melt the butter in a thick-based saucepan or casserole dish and gently cook and soften the onions for 5 mins in the butter or until pale gold. Remove them to a plate with a slotted spoon. Turn the heat up high, add the pieces of meat a few at a time and brown them. Reduce the heat, return the onion and all the meat to the pan, season and pour in the wine or cider (I prefer the wine) and if you allow for a bit extra you can have a drink whilst cooking!

2 Bring to simmering point, cover and let it cook very gently on top of the stove for about 1½ hours. Stir occasionally. Tip – this recipe can easily be adapted for the AGA (or oven), by putting the pan or casserole dish into the simmering oven once the dish has been brought to simmering point.

3 Then stir in the mushrooms (which will add a lot of juice in case you think it seems a little dry). Put the lid back on and leave to cook very gently for a further 30 mins or until the meat is tender.

4 Taste for seasoning and stir in the cream with a good grating of fresh nutmeg. Let the cream heat through.

Serve with plain or wild rice and some good French bread. Garnish with parsley.

Serves: 3-4
- 700g (1½lbs) venison
- 2 large onions
- 56g (2oz) butter
- 300ml (10fl oz) dry white wine or cider
- 500g (1lb) mushrooms, sliced
- 300ml (10fl oz) soured cream (or double cream)
- Freshly grated nutmeg
- Salt and freshly ground pepper

Tip – Any cut of venison can be used for this recipe with an adjustment on cooking times. The time suggested is not for the best cuts. If using better cuts, choose the haunch (leg) and reduce your cooking time by half and even more if using the best meat from the loin (saddle) area.

Country Flavours

"Our free range egg company is based at Lower Bellamoor Farms where my family have been based for four generations... so far. As with many small farms we have looked for areas in which we can diversify, and apart from free range eggs we also supply fruit jellies and fruit juices; but our brown hens are the centre of our universe and eggs laid one day can be on someone's breakfast table the next morning. Little known is the fact that eggs contain every vitamin apart from vitamin C, as well as important antioxidants. Studies have also shown that eating eggs for breakfast can even help you lose weight! Most importantly our hens are happy Herefordshire hens which helps make our eggs some of the best!" **Alice Hancorn**

Serves: 2-4
- 8 Country Flavours free range eggs
- 4 medium Herefordshire potatoes, thinly sliced
- 1 dash olive oil
- 1 onion
- 1 clove garlic
- 1 red pepper
- 100g (4oz) local goat's cheese
- Salt and freshly ground pepper

Herefordshire Tortilla

1 Fry the potatoes, onion and garlic in the olive oil until tender. Then thinly slice the peppers and add to pan.

2 Whisk the eggs together with some salt and pepper. Pour the eggs into the pan and sprinkle on the goat's cheese. (We used Neal's Yard Creamery, Ragstone).

3 As the egg cooks, pull away from the edges slightly and allow the uncooked egg to get to the edge.

4 To finish, pop under a grill to cook the top (alternatively, turn out onto a plate to turn the tortilla over and return to the pan, reduce the heat to finish cooking).

Serve with Country Flavours onion relish, for a quick lunch or comforting supper.

Broadfield Court & Bodenham English Wines

"I always wondered why Broadfield had vines, and one Sunday afternoon, I plucked up the courage to ask! What I thought was an innocuous question turned out to be a revelation. Keith James, my father-in-law was a soldier in the Second World War, and became a prisoner of war in Italy. After digging an escape tunnel using a single silver spoon, he made his way to the nearest farm. Weighing only six stone, he implored the owners to take him in, which they agreed to on one condition – that he pruned their vines. So, Keith owed his life to his vines, and his passion for growing was passed on to me. Whenever I can, I use our wine in cooking and to serve with meals, as it is always such a special treat to drink wine that has come from Herefordshire. Accompanying the wine with pheasant and vegetables from our very own estate, there is nothing better in the cold winter months than a simple warming supper from your own back door!" **Alex James**

Pheasant and Prune Casserole

1 Chop the pheasant breasts into strips and dust in seasoned flour. Add a knob of butter and a dash of oil to a large casserole pan. Add the onions and garlic and gently fry until translucent, approx. 10 mins.

2 Add the pheasant breasts and pitted prunes, along with the herbs and seasoning, and fry until browned. Add the stock and Broadfield Court rosé wine. Let simmer for 20 mins. Stir in the double cream to finish, and remove from the heat.

3 Grill thin pancetta slices on a baking sheet with parchment paper below and on top, until crispy. Arrange on top of the casserole, with some of the chopped herbs.

Serve with creamy celeriac mash and seasonal greens, as a quick, warming supper. Enjoy with a delicious glass of Broadfield Court rosé wine.

Serves: 6-8
- 6 pheasant breasts
- 2 onions, diced
- 1 clove of garlic, finely diced
- 1 tablespoon plain flour
- 20 pitted prunes
- Fresh thyme, chopped
- Fresh parsley, chopped
- Fresh chervil, chopped
- 3 tablespoons double cream
- 275ml (½ pint) chicken or pheasant stock
- 150ml (¼ pint) Broadfield Court rosé wine
- 1 knob of butter
- 1 dash of oil
- Salt and freshly ground pepper

Golden Valley Goats

"Our story begins nearly ten years ago with the wife's desire to keep a couple of pet goats. Our lack of space coupled with a reluctant husband and two young children saw this idea put on the back burner to gather dust. Fast forward ten very hectic years and our situation looks very different – our young children are not quite so young, a house move granted us a little more space and the reluctant husband discovers goats are not so bad after all. Now we're here in Herefordshire supplying goat milk, goat meat, fresh goat's cheese and even goat milk fudge, to local shops and farmers markets. There are many health benefits to goat milk – it is easy to digest, contains less lactose and is delicious. The meat is very tasty too, and this is our favourite goat curry recipe. Enjoy!" **Rob and Miriam Roberts**

Aromatic Goat Curry

1 Pulse all of the ingredients for the paste in a food processor until evenly chopped. This provides the base for the curry.

2 Combine all the rest of the ingredients with the paste, in a slow cooker. Cook for 6-7 hours, stirring occasionally until very tender.

3 Turn the heat off and allow the curry to rest for about a quarter of an hour.

Serve with rice. Sprinkle over some coriander leaves and lime juice, if desired.

Serves: 4
- 1kg diced goat meat
- 120ml (4fl oz) water
- 200ml (7fl oz) coconut milk
- 3 teaspoons ground coriander
- 2 teaspoons ground cumin
- ½ teaspoon turmeric
- 3 star anise
- 1 tablespoon sugar
- 1 teaspoon salt

For the paste:
- 40g (1½oz) lightly toasted desiccated coconut
- 1 brown onion
- 2 tablespoon chopped fresh ginger
- 6 cloves garlic
- 2 sweet red chillies
- Zest of 1 lime
- 1 small bunch coriander stems

onion

garlic

Pixley Berries

"At Pixley, we are almost as crazy about bumblebees as we are about blackcurrants. Bumblebees at Pixley seem to particularly love the flowers on our 'Pixley Black' blackcurrants that go into the cordial which flavours this lamb recipe – we should have called it Pixley Bumble. Did you know that Herefordshire bumblebees can visit patches of flowers over 1 mile from their colony and while foraging, bumblebees can reach ground speeds of up to 15 metres per second (that's over 30 miles an hour) – great for all our blackcurrant plantations and varieties. My all-time favourite of our juice concoctions is a glass of Pixley Court 'Blackcurrant, Apple and Rhubarb'. It keeps me off the wine – although some say a little late!" **Edward Thompson**

Pixley Roast Lamb with Italian Beans

1 Using a sharp knife, cut small slashes all over the lamb then push a slice of garlic into each. Put half the thyme, 3 tablespoons olive oil, Pixley Berries Blackcurrant Cordial, wine, lemon zest and a good grinding of black pepper into a large freezer bag. Add the lamb, tie the bag tightly and refrigerate for at least four hours, preferably overnight.

2 Heat oven to 220°C (425°F, Gas Mark 7). Put the rest of the thyme into the bottom of a roasting tin then lift the lamb out of the marinade and sit on top of the thyme. Roast for 20 mins, then toss onions into the tin, drizzle with a little oil, then turn the oven down to 190°C (375°F, Gas Mark 5). Roast for 15 mins per 450g (1lb) for medium.

3 Meanwhile strain the marinade into a pan, add most of the stock and boil until reduced by two thirds (this should take around 20 mins). Set aside in a jug. The gravy can be made ahead or the day before if necessary, as long as the meat has marinated for at least four hours.

4 Once the lamb is ready, take out and rest on a board, wrapped in a tent of foil to keep warm. Set the onions aside in a bowl. Put the roasting tin onto the hob on a low heat and pour in the balsamic vinegar with a splash more stock and scrape all the meaty bits from the bottom. Tip this mixture into the jug with the gravy.

5 For the beans, add 2 tablespoons olive oil to the roasting tin. Add the rosemary and tomatoes and fry for 1 minute until the rosemary smells aromatic. Tip in the beans, the red onions and the final splash of stock then warm through. Season. Then stir in the parsley just before serving.

Serve on a platter, topped with the lamb. Enjoy with a glass of Pixley Court 'Blackcurrant, Apple and Rhubarb'.

Serves: 6-8
- 2 kg (4lb 6oz) leg of lamb (Ryeland preferably)
- 4 cloves garlic, sliced
- 8 sprigs fresh thyme
- 5 tablespoons olive oil
- 5 tablespoons Pixley Berries Blackcurrant Cordial
- Half a bottle of red wine
- Zest of 1 lemon
- 1 litre (1¾ pints) lamb stock
- 3 red onions, cut into 6 wedges
- 3 tablespoons balsamic vinegar

For the beans:
- 2 sprigs rosemary, roughly chopped
- 110g (4oz) sunblush tomatoes
- 1.2kg (2lb 10oz) cannellini beans
- Handful of flatleaf parsley, roughly chopped
- Salt and freshly ground pepper

The Orgasmic Cider Co

"As we sit under our leafy apple trees contemplating some of the earliest pints of cider ever made, and sip our own smooth brew we are just a little sad for John the Baptist. The Wycliffe 'Cider' Bible, printed in the early 15th Century is kept in Hereford Cathedral's Chained Library gives us the classic verse 'For he (John the Baptist) shall be great in the sight of the Lord, and shall drink neither wine nor sidir...'. We are not sure whether our family were making cider in the 15th Century, but we have restarted a family tradition of four generations of cider and perry producers. And thanks to our local pub in Winforton, The Sun Inn, we came up with our sophisticated pork, apricot and Orgasmic Cider pie, which must be accompanied by a smooth Orgasmic pint!" **Stephen Layton**

Pork, Apricot and Orgasmic Cider Pie with Black Pudding Mash and Baby Leeks

1 First make the pastry. Put the flour, salt, butter and the lard in to a large bowl. Using your fingertips rub the fat into the flour until you have a mixture that resembles breadcrumbs. Using a knife, stir in just enough cold water to bind the dough together. Wrap in cling film and chill until needed.

2 To make the pie filling add the butter to a large pan, fry the onions and celery for 5 mins until cooked, add the herbs and garlic and cook for a further 2-3 mins. Add the pork to the pan and fry until brown, pour in the cider and chicken stock and cook for 2 hours or until tender. Pour in the double cream and reduce for 20 mins then season. Leave to cool.

3 Pour the pie filling in to a pie dish. Roll out the pastry on a floured surface, put over the top of the pie dish, crimp the edges and brush with a beaten egg. Bake on 180°C (350°F, Gas Mark 4) until golden brown.

4 For the black pudding mash, peel and chop the potatoes put in a pan and cover with water then season with salt. Boil until cooked, then mash them. Add the black pudding, cream, and butter. Season with salt and pepper. Keep warm until needed.

5 Boil a pan of seasoned water, add the leeks and cook for 4-5 mins.

Plate up and sprinkle with a little thyme, for an Orgasmic meal!

Serves: 6
For the pastry:
- 500g (1lb 2oz) plain flour
- 125g (4½oz) butter
- 125g (4½oz) lard
- 1 pinch of salt

For the filling:
- 1kg (2lb 3oz) pork shoulder, diced
- 1 onion, diced
- 2 sticks celery, diced
- 2 cloves of garlic, crushed
- 1 tablespoon mixed herbs
- 150g (5oz) butter
- 1 bottle of Orgasmic Cider
- 500g (1lb 2oz) dried apricots
- 855ml (1½ pints) chicken stock
- 1.2 litres (2 pints) double cream

For the black pudding mash:
- 1kg (2lb 3oz) potatoes
- 300g (10½oz) black pudding
- 150ml (¼ pint) double cream
- 100g (3½oz) butter

- 12 baby leeks

The Kilpeck Inn

"We're very lucky to have the award winning chef, Ross Williams, in our kitchen. He fully supports our mantra of using local Herefordshire produce whenever possible. There is nothing better than knowing that your meat is from the local farmer and your cider is freshly pressed in a nearby orchard. All good pubs should be the heartbeat to their village and I hope we are going some way to making this metaphor a reality. It's a great place to stop after you have enjoyed the incredible Norman stone carvings in our village church, built in 1140. Having examined the 85 corbels outside and inside the church with their representations of hares, fish, fowl and stags what better place to come to sample dishes of the same!" **Julian Vaughan**

Slow Roasted Pork Belly with Black Pudding Stuffed Tenderloin, Apple Mash, Braised Red Cabbage and Cider Gravy

1 For the pork belly, preheat the oven to 160°C, (320°F, Gas Mark 3). Roughly chop the vegetables and place in a large deep roasting tray together with the bay leaves, star anise and peppercorns. Place the pork belly on top of the vegetables and fill up to half way with cold water. Place a sheet of baking parchment over the top and seal with tin foil. Place in the oven and cook for 3 hours, or until the pork is tender. Remove the pork and allow to cool, discarding the vegetables but reserving the liquor for the cider gravy. Score the skin and put under a hot grill until golden brown.

2 For the tenderloin, trim any excess fat or sinew from the pork and slice three quarters of the way through to form a pocket along the length of the tenderloin. Crumble or mash the black pudding and stuff inside the pork then wrap with the pancetta or bacon. Sear the tenderloin in a hot, lightly oiled pan then transfer to a hot oven for 15 mins. Allow to rest for 10 mins then carve into slices.

3 For the cider gravy, bring the pork belly liquor and cider to the boil in a saucepan, add the gravy powder and reduce to the required consistency.

4 For the apple mash, peel and roughly chop the apple and place in a saucepan with a splash of water. Cook until the apple has broken down then blend or mash to create a smooth apple sauce. Peel and roughly chop the potatoes and boil in salted water until soft. Drain, add the butter and mash until smooth. Stir the apple sauce into the mashed potato.

5 For the braised red cabbage, cut the cabbage into quarters and remove the woody stem. Thinly slice and place into a saucepan with the rest of the ingredients. Cover and simmer for 45 mins, or until the cabbage is tender. Remove the lid and continue to simmer until the liquid has reduced by around half.

Arrange a slice of the pork belly, three rings of the tenderloin with the apple mash and braised red cabbage, on a warmed plate, drizzle the cider gravy and garnish with a sprig of sage.

Serves: 4

For the pork belly:
- 1 pork belly (bones removed)
- 4 carrots
- ½ head celery
- 2 onions
- 2 leeks
- 2 heads fennel
- 4 bay leaves
- 8 star anise
- Handful of black peppercorns

For the tenderloin:
- 1 pork tenderloin
- 1 stick of black pudding or boudin noir
- Sliced pancetta or thinly sliced smoked streaky bacon

For the cider gravy:
- Reserved pork belly liquor
- 570ml (1 pint) dry cider
- 1 tablespoon good quality gravy powder

For the apple mash:
- 1 Bramley apple
- 1kg (2lbs 3oz) Maris Pipers (or similar floury potatoes)
- 100g (3½oz) butter
- Salt and freshly ground pepper

For the braised red cabbage:
- 1 head red cabbage
- 100ml (3½fl oz) red wine
- 100ml (3½fl oz) balsamic vinegar
- 100g (3½oz) light soft brown sugar
- 1 tablespoon redcurrant jelly

Hopes of Longtown

"We all have our most loved family dishes and here in the Black Mountains one of our favourite dishes for all year round is shepherd's pie. You may think shepherd's pie is just a winter warmer but we believe it is a delicious dish worthy of eating by roaring fires in the winter and under the shade of trees in the summer. In old and well thumbed cook books you won't find weights, temperatures and measures, it's all about finding, tasting, adapting and developing recipes to suit what's in season and your taste buds. First known of in 1877 and originally for using up the left over roast, shepherd's pie still is a simple but delicious dish, and ours even simpler as our recipe comes with no measurements either. We suggest you have fun and adapt this recipe for the season you are eating in." **Christine Hope**

Core ingredients:
- Butter
- Red onion (brown is fine too)
- Forage Fine Foods pontack
- Lamb mince (or left over Sunday roast cuts)
- Potatoes
- Whole milk
- Coarse sea salt

Pontack, one of our favourite sauces, is a spicy elderberry reduction.

Seasonal Shepherd's Pie

1 Peel and chop the potatoes, add them to a saucepan of boiling water, and simmer.

2 Meanwhile, place a knob of butter in a frying pan to melt. Chop the red onion, place in the pan and fry gently. Once softened, place in a pie dish. In the same frying pan, gently cook the lamb mince, add the pontack (or a seasonal sauce of your choice), to keep the mince moist. Simmer, and add to the dish.

3 Take potatoes off the heat, drain and mash, adding whole milk and butter to suit. Put the mash on top of your meat base and score with a fork adding course sea salt on the top. Put in a preheated oven until golden.

Seasonal adaptations
Spring – Try layering (between the meat and potato) spring greens, chard, nettle tips and kale.
Summer – In early summer mint is at its best (add to the meat sauce), and the first crops of broad beans, peas or ground elder. Try replacing the whole milk with goat's milk and in late summer take advantage of gluts of tomatoes and courgettes.
Autumn – Blackberries for a fruity twist, leeks, pumpkins and butternut squash.
Winter – Celeriac, parsnip, swede, jerusalem artichoke either add a middle layer or mix with the potato topping or replace the potato topping entirely.

Seasonal side dishes
Spring – Steamed leeks and black pepper.
Summer – Mixed leaf salad with Rosehip and Horseradish sauce (we like Forage Fine Foods).
Autumn – Buttered corn on the cob.
Winter – Slow cooked red cabbage and apple in red wine with cinnamon.

Delectable desserts
and sweet treats

Bearwood Bees

"Across North Herefordshire, our beehives are situated in wildflower meadows, ancient woodland and fruit orchards. Our love of beekeeping and bees has grown from a hobby and we are now a family of beekeepers, committed to looking after these fascinating insects, who play such an important part in the pollination of our local fruit harvests. Collecting nectar from the abundant local blossom, including orchard apple, wild cherry and bramble, they supply us with light and delicious honey. Bees have to fly about 55,000 miles and need to visit over two million flowers to make just one pound of honey, so we think that they probably know more about our lovely county than any other creature!" **Suzanne Wenczek**

Honey Fudge

1 Put all the ingredients together in a large, heavy-bottomed pan, over a gentle heat. Keep stirring until the mixture starts to bubble.

2 Turn the heat up to medium-high heat and keep stirring to prevent sticking. Be patient and cook for several mins until it reaches 115°C (240°F) on a sugar thermometer or 'soft-ball' stage. If you don't have a sugar thermometer, test the set by dropping a little of the mixture into cold water. If it forms a ball, it is ready.

3 Cool the pan quickly by standing in cold water. Beat the mixture with a wooden spoon until it begins to thicken. Pour into a tin lined with greaseproof paper and allow to cool and set before cutting into squares.

Apparently this fudge keeps really well, but it never lasts long enough in this house to test the theory!

Makes: **24 pieces**
- 450g (1lb) granulated sugar
- 150ml (5oz) evaporated milk
- 65g (2¼oz) salted butter
- 3 tablespoons honey (runny or set, but the darker the better)
- 1 good pinch of cream of tartar

Ye Olde Steppes

"In early 2012, we renovated and re-opened Ye Olde Steppes, a 500 year old black and white building. Although we had no experience in retail or catering (I was a clinical nurse specialist with a penchant for home baking and Mark was a senior academic in IT) the rule book was thrown to the wind. Thoughts and ideas on how Ye Olde Steppes could be reborn were gathered from the history of the building and thoughts and ideas from the villagers. Mark is often found on the counter in the shop or taming the tea gardens whilst I bake up experimental cakes using local produce and flavours that stir memories of home." **Gary Seaton**

Serves: **8**

For the cake:
- 3 large Country Flavour's eggs
- Calon Wen Organic salted butter
- Wessex Mill self-raising flour
- Caster sugar
- 150ml (¼ pint) Dunkerton's Black Fox Cider
- 175g (6oz) sultanas
- 2 large Herefordshire Bramley apples
- 1 teaspoon cinnamon
- 1 teaspoon nutmeg

For the crumbly topping:
- 75g (3oz) self-raising flour
- 25g (1oz) Calon Wen Organic salted butter
- 50g (2oz) demerara sugar
- 50g (2oz) flaked almonds

Apple Cider Cake with Crumbly Almond Topping

1 Start by cracking open the cider. Pour half the bottle into a saucepan and add the sultanas. Drink the rest of the bottle. Simmer the sultanas in the cider for 10-15 mins until they look plump and cider filled. Drain your sultanas and allow to cool. Keep the thickened cider syrup to one side for later.

2 Weigh your three eggs in their shells. Write down the weight and weigh out equal amounts of caster sugar, softened butter and flour. Whisk your eggs in a bowl and set aside. In your mixing bowl cream the butter and caster sugar until light in colour and texture. Add your whisked eggs slowly, being careful not to curdle the mixture (if the mixture looks like it may be separating add a teaspoon of the self-raising flour). Sift the flour, nutmeg and cinnamon onto the mixture and mix, folding until combined.

3 Peel, core and chop the Bramley apples into chunks, about 1cm in size. Fold the apple chunks and cider soaked sultanas into the cake mix. Spatula the mix into a greased 30cm (12 inch) spring form cake tin (using two strips of greaseproof paper makes it easier to get the cake out of the tin!).

4 In a separate bowl add the 75g of flour and 25g of softened butter. Rub the butter into the flour with your fingers until the mix resembles bread crumbs. Throw in the demerara sugar and mix. Now, add to the crumble a few tablespoons of the cider syrup created from soaking the sultanas. Mix with a spoon or your fingers until the mix looks crumble-like in appearance. Add the crumble topping to the top of the cake and evenly sprinkle the flaked almonds.

5 Cook at 170°C (325°F, Gas Mark 3) for 45 mins or until a skewer comes out clean.

Serve either chilled with a nice cup of tea or warmed through with a big dollop of clotted cream. Yum!

Court Farm & Leisure

"We produce over 40 types of fruit and vegetables in beautiful rolling Herefordshire countryside, but we are probably best known for our magnificent English Cherries. We grow more than 20 varieties so spreading the harvest availability from the end of June to the middle of August. Our family business has been here for over 30 years supplying locally through 'Pick Your Own', a well-stocked farm shop and wonderful tea room. And to keep the family entertained the younger family members can meet all our farm animals and even PYO chicken eggs. For the more daredevil members of the family we even offer the only destination in Herefordshire for mountain boarding!" **Nicki Gilbert**

Serves: 8

For the pastry:
- 85g (3oz) plain flour
- 30g (1¼oz) ground almonds
- 55g (2oz) cool unsalted butter, diced
- 25g (1oz) icing sugar, sifted
- 1 egg yolk
- 1 tablespoon cold water

For the filling:
- 700g (1lb 8oz) cherries, pitted
- 100g (3½oz) brown sugar
- Zest of 1 orange
- 1 vanilla pod, split and seeded
- 100g (3½oz) dark chocolate, smashed
- 1 tablespoon cornflour
- 1 tablespoon whole milk
- 1 tablespoon golden caster sugar

Ultimate Cherry Pie

1 For the pastry, sift the flour into a mixing bowl. Add the ground almonds and butter and rub in until the mixture resembles fine breadcrumbs. Stir in the sugar.

2 Beat the egg yolk with the cold water. Add to the flour mixture and mix in with a round-bladed knife. Gather together to make a soft dough. Don't over-mix. Wrap in cling film and chill for at least 30 mins before rolling out.

3 Heat the oven to 180°C (350°F, Gas Mark 4). Roll out just over half the pastry and line a 23cm (9 inch) pie dish. Cover the pastry with baking parchment and baking beans, and bake for 10 mins. Take out the paper and beans, and cook for 5 mins. Set to the side to cool.

4 Increase the oven to 200°C (400°F, Gas Mark 6). Mix the cherries with the sugar, orange zest and vanilla seeds, in a baking dish, and cover with foil. Bake for 30 mins. Remove from the oven and drain off the juice into a saucepan. Cool the fruit.

5 Mix the cornflour with 3 tablespoons of the juice, and stir back into the juice in the pan. Bring to a simmer, and cook until it thickens, into a smooth sauce. Allow to cool.

6 Put the fruit in the pie base and pour over some of the sauce. Add the chocolate pieces evenly over the fruit. Roll out the rest of the pastry, cut strips and arrange over the top in a lattice effect.

7 Brush with milk and scatter with sugar. Decrease the oven temperature back to 180°C (350°F, Gas Mark 4), and bake for 20 mins, or until golden. Add a foil collar if the edge is going too brown.

Serve with the extra sauce and a scoop of local goat milk ice cream (we used Q Goats from Tillington).

Once Upon a Tree

"As huge food and drink enthusiasts, we founded our small company with Ann and Norman Stanier in 2007, bringing together the skills of an experienced winemaker and exceptional orchardist to produce an innovative range of ciders and perries. It is always a joy to use great local ingredients in cooking, and we have re-connected the link between good cider and good food, which was always our intention and something that seemed to be missing 10 years ago. We are proud to say that this collaborative approach has been embraced by our customers, as well as being recognised in numerous competitions." **Simon and Hannah Day**

Poached Pears with The Wonder Pear Syllabub

1 For the poached pears, add the Priggles Perry to a medium sized saucepan and bring to simmering with the sugar and the cinnamon. Peel the pears and add to the saucepan. Make sure the pears are completely covered (add a touch of water if not). Cover with a baking paper cartouche and gently poach until the pears are soft, about 20-30 mins depending on the ripeness of your pears. These can be made well ahead of time and chilled in the poaching liquor in the fridge.

2 Remove the pears and set aside to cool. Continue to boil the liquid until it has reduced by half and is nice and syrupy.

3 For the syllabub, gently heat The Wonder with the sugar and cinnamon, until the sugar is dissolved and the flavours are infused – be careful not to boil! Leave to cool completely.

4 In a large bowl whip the cream, gradually incorporating the cooled liquid, until soft peaks start to form. Stop whisking as soon as the syllabub just holds its shape, but is not too thick.

5 Stand each pear on a plate (you may need to chop a little from the bottom), add a spoonful of the syllabub, a drizzle of the reduced perry syrup and a sprinkle of grated chocolate.

Serve with a chilled glass of The Wonder!

Serves: **4**

For the Pears:
- 4 pears
- 4 tablespoons sugar
- 500ml (17½fl oz) Priggles Perry
- 1 pinch ground cinnamon

For the Syllabub:
- 200ml (7fl oz) The Wonder dessert pear wine
- 50g (2oz) sugar
- Pinch ground cinnamon
- 600ml (21fl oz) double cream
- 1 sprinkle of grated dark chocolate

The Wonder is a dessert pear ice-wine made by freeze concentrating Conference and Comice pear juice, and stopping the fermentation to yield a sweet, balanced dessert wine, with hints of apricot, quince and melon.

Priggles Perry is a blend of traditional perry pear varieties, fermented in cool conditions. With melon and lemon blossom on the nose and ripe pear flavours on the palate.

little pear

Rayeesa's Indian Kitchen

"I moved to Herefordshire 7 years ago from a busy London lifestyle. Here I rediscovered my childhood passion for my mother's and grandmother's delicious Indian food. Both for making, eating and sharing with others. It was this passion that inspired me to open my Indian cookery school, set in our idyllic Herefordshire farmhouse kitchen, the perfect combination of East meets West. Far removed from my former life as a police woman, living in the undulating riverine area of Mordiford I have found a different pace of life – quite different from what life is like for some of my cousins who live in the hustle and noise of Hyderabad. How lucky I am to have found Herefordshire and to be able to use such fabulous local produce." **Rayeesa Asghar-Sandys**

Serves: 4
- 350g (12oz) caster sugar
- 3-4 green cardamom pods
- 2 teaspoons rosewater
- 400g (14oz) powdered milk
- 200g (7oz) self-raising flour
- 2 green apples diced
- 3 tablespoons vegetable oil
- 100ml (3½fl oz) milk
- Vegetable oil for frying
- 1 sprinkle pistachios, roughly chopped (optional)

Apple Gulab Jamun
(Milk Dough Balls Stuffed with Apples, Soaked in Cardamom and Rosewater Syrup)

1 First make your syrup by bringing 1litre (1¾ pints) of water to boil in a heavy based pan. Then add 300g (10oz) of the sugar, cardamom pods and rosewater, stirring constantly until it dissolves. Reduce the heat and simmer until the syrup has reduced by half.

2 In a bowl mix the flour and powdered milk and add the 3 tablespoons of oil to make fine breadcrumbs. Stir in the milk to make elastic dough with the milk and flour mixture (be careful not to have too dry a mixture). Knead it until smooth. Then keep aside covered for ½-1 hour.

3 For the filling simply steam the diced apples in their own juices in a heavy based pan with 50g (2oz) of sugar. When slightly cooked remove with a slotted spoon and allow to cool.

4 On a lightly floured surface, roll into small balls about 3cm in diameter. Using your thumb and fingers make a small cup shape, fill with a few pieces of the stewed apples. Cover over the dough over the apple filling making sure that there are no gaps and gently roll back into a ball. Make as many as you can and set aside.

5 Heat the oil in a frying pan, reduce to low/medium heat and start frying the balls in batches of 4-5 at a time. Keep moving them while they fry to ensure they cook evenly. Remove them when they turn a lovely dark brown and put onto some kitchen paper.

6 When they are all cooked add the balls to the syrup and let them soak for 20 mins.

Serve hot or cold, garnished with pistachio and crème fraîche. And why not try with a sprinkling of some Sweet Rose Dukkah (a magical blend of roses and spices by Forage Fine Foods). Enjoy!

Sue Gilmour Chocolates

"Loving my garden as I do, it was a natural step to add botanical flavours to my delicious chocolate. Did you know, for example, that lavender comes from the same family as mint, so it's not surprising that it works so well with chocolate. The rich Herefordshire countryside is so steeped in wild and cultivated herbs and botanicals that it is easy to pursue my passion for both chocolate and gardening – I don't have to wander far from my Bromyard home to find the natural ingredients to use in my original handmade chocolates. This simple, classic recipe always goes down a storm at dinner parties, it allows the flavours within the chocolate to really sing, and it so easy to prepare!" **Sue Gilmour**

Serves: **6**
- 200g (7oz) Sue Gilmour Lavender Dark Chocolate
- 160ml (5½fl oz) cream
- 75ml (3fl oz) milk
- 2 egg yolks

Lavender Chocolate Pots

1 Place 6 expresso cups in the fridge to chill. Chop the chocolate into small pieces (don't forget there's always a small taste for the chef!).

2 Heat the cream and milk in a saucepan over a medium heat. Remove from the heat just as it starts to boil. Add the chocolate and stir until the chocolate is completely melted.

3 Whisk the eggs yolks into the mixture, and pour into the chilled expresso cups. Set in the fridge to chill for at least 4 hours.

Serve topped with just a sprinkle of lavender flowers.

lavender

The Garden Tea Room & Deli

"Our Tea Room and Deli have been open since 2010, and although every minute is hard work, every minute is enjoyed as much as the last! The reward we find in inventing delicious new recipes cannot be underestimated. We were concerned that using our house would intrude on our lives, but not only has it opened a vintage home for all to see but we also get meet so many fascinating people who are touring this nook of the county. We have discovered some wonderful old family recipes, to which we give a fresh modern twist, making eating in our house a very special experience. The Garden is also the home of 'Jenny Lee Teas' a national fundraising initiative where people pledge to host afternoon teas and raise money for grass roots community projects in Herefordshire and beyond, and so as well as tickling taste buds we are also putting something back in." **Joanna Bruce**

The Garden Summer Fruit Flan

1 For the flan base, preheat the oven to 170°C (325°F, Gas Mark 3). Grease a loose-bottomed flan tin.

2 Weigh out all the dry ingredients into a bowl. Break the eggs into a jug and blend together with a fork. Pour the eggs into the dry ingredients and mix fully until you have a wet sloppy texture.

3 Pour into the flan tin and bake in the middle of the oven until firm to touch. Leave in the tin and place on a wire rack to cool. Carefully ease out of the tin and turn right side up.

4 To decorate, make sure the flan base is completely cold. Spread the top with a thin layer of lemon curd. Cover with a generous layer of crème fraîche. Decorate with a scattering of sliced strawberries, whole raspberries and blueberries. Keep refrigerated until you serve.

Serves: **6-8**
- 200g (7oz) demerara sugar
- 250g (9oz) ground hazelnuts or almonds
- 8 free range bantam eggs
- 1 teaspoon 'gluten free' baking powder
- 2 tablespoons lemon curd
- 250g (9oz) low fat crème fraîche
- 300g (10½oz) mixed seasonal berries (e.g. strawberries, raspberries and blueberries)

Lower Hope Fruit

"As a boy, I used to come to Herefordshire with my family to pick blackberries. Years later I returned to establish a large farming estate in Ullingswick. Today, standing at 800 feet above sea level, our orchards provide panoramic views across the beautiful Herefordshire countryside. Our first cherry orchard was harvested in 1998 yielding 10 tonnes of fruit. Now we harvest approximately 400 tonnes and are one of the leading UK cherry growers supplying both nationally and locally. The British cherry saw a steady decline post war when traditional orchards became unsustainable. From the early 1990's Lower Hope led the way in the revival of British cherry growing introducing new rootstock and tree management, along with the addition of rain covers. This gives consistency of quality and enables us to pick the juiciest, sweetest and biggest cherries straight from the tree." **Clive Richards**

Cherry Clafoutis

1 Preheat oven to 200°C (400°F, Gas Mark 6). Lightly grease the baking dish, and spread the cherries evenly over the base.

2 Place the flour and caster sugar in a mixing bowl and combine. Lightly beat the eggs and combine into the flour. Then, mix in the sugar.

3 Combine the milk, vanilla and butter, then pour into the egg mixture and beat until combined into a batter.

4 Carefully pour the batter over the cherries in the baking dish and place in the oven until the clafoutis is golden brown. This will take approx. 30 mins.

Once the clafoutis is golden brown leave to cool, then serve warm or cold, dusted with icing sugar.

Serves: 8
- 500g (1lb 2oz) cherries, pitted
- 60g (2½oz) plain flour
- 90g (3½oz) caster sugar
- 2 eggs
- 200ml (7fl oz) milk
- 1 teaspoon vanilla extract
- 20g (¾oz) butter, melted
- 1 dusting of icing sugar

cherries

Frome Valley Vineyard

"Coming to vineyards and wine-making as a total novice, I am still astonished how very different every year is from the last; how each grape variety makes a wine so characteristically itself but so distinctive from year to year; how wine develops in the bottle over the years; how much difference 'terroir' really does make. We are extraordinarily lucky where we are. Our four acre vineyard is set amongst Herefordshire's hop yards and cider orchards in the beautiful meandering Frome valley. Our microclimate lets us grow and (importantly!) ripen Pinot Noir and Seyval Blanc for our rose and sparkling wines and another six varieties for our other single variety and blended wines. Having had a 200-year odd break from vines after their introduction to Britain by the Romans, Herefordshire is rapidly becoming a centre for the revival of English wine. And we're part of it! Very exciting!" **Jeanie Falconer**

Paunton Syllabub

Serves: **4**
- 1 glass of Paunton Medium Dry
- 200ml double cream
- A spoonful of sugar (a teaspoon if you're sweet enough already; a dessert spoon if you need more!)

1 Put all the ingredients into a bowl. Whisk until the cream turns firm and holds its shape. Put into ramekins or individual glass dishes and chill in the fridge for an hour.

2 Serve (we served ours topped with blackcurrants in British Cassis and a sprinkle of lime zest!).

Why not start your meal with a little Paunton magic too…
Try a Paunton Kir Royal… put a drop or two of British Cassis into the bottom of a champagne glass, fill to the top with chilled Paunton Sparkling. Et voila! the world's most delicious aperitif!

… grapes

Wye Valley Brewery

"When we were asked to come up with a recipe we asked the daughter of a local hop grower – Dorothy Goodbody. She certainly has her head screwed on, and only puts her name to the purest ales and the very best cakes! Here Dorothy has used her award winning and wonderfully sumptuous wholesome stout to create this luxurious chocolate cake. This recipe has been kept secret until now, but Dorothy felt it was time to share it with others. Enjoy!" **Vernon Amor**

Dorothy Goodbody's Luxurious Chocolate Cake

1 Preheat oven to 180°C (350°F, Gas Mark 4). Line a 19cm (7.5 inch) springform tin, with greased baking paper.

2 Cream the butter and sugar together in a large mixing bowl, or kitchen mixer. Add the eggs gradually, and beat until pale and fluffy.

3 Sift flour, bicarbonate and baking powder into a separate bowl. In another bowl or jug, slowly mix the beer into the cocoa.

4 Alternately add the cocoa mix and the flour mix in small quantities into the butter, sugar, egg mix and combine well.

5 Pour into the lined tin, and bake for about one hour (until a wooden skewer inserted into the middle comes out clean).

6 Leave to cool. If you are not going to eat it immediately, either clingfilm the cake once it has cooled, or store in an airtight tin.

7 For the sauce, warm the chocolate and cream slowly together in a heavy bottomed pan on a medium heat.

8 Take off the heat before the chocolate has quite finished melting. Stir to a silky smoothness. The sauce is ready to serve now or it can be saved and reheated later.

Serves: 8

For the cake:
- 125g (4oz) unsalted butter
- 275g (9oz) dark soft brown sugar
- 2 eggs, beaten
- 170g (6oz) plain flour
- ½ teaspoon baking powder
- 1 teaspoon bicarbonate of soda
- 200 ml (7fl oz) Dorothy Goodbody's Wholesome Stout
- 75g (3oz) cocoa powder

For the chocolate sauce:
- 150g (6oz) chocolate
- 250 ml (10fl oz) double cream

chocolate

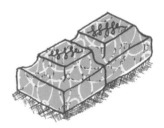

Mayfields Brewery

"We pride ourselves on being artisan brewers of cask and bottle conditioned 'beers of character'! We filter our brewing water so it's pure and use only the finest 'Maris Otter' malts and whole hops, many of which are grown locally. This careful handcrafting of quality ingredients creates a variety of beers from our dark and delicious BV Stout, through to our light Hoppy Priory Pale Ale. After meeting Liz Knight at a food showcase at Hopes of Longtown, she started experimenting by combining our bitter, deep and malty ales with her delicious sweet syrups. And so, with a bit of playing, two polar opposite flavours from Herefordshire came together in a joyful experiment, with our chocolate and coffee flavoured BV Stout and her delicate sweet rose syrup (an old fashioned syrup made with rose petals gathered from lovely gardens around south Herefordshire) resulting in this classic, sweet dish." **Adam Smith**

BV Stout and Rose Tiramisu

1 Whisk together the egg yolks with half of the sugar until it is light and fluffy, fold in the mascarpone a third at a time – whisking to combine them, add the rose petal preserve and whisk until the syrup is blended with the cream.

2 Beat the egg whites and the remainder of the sugar to soft peaks, then gently fold into the egg yolk mixture. Spread one third of the mixture over the bottom of your tiramisu dish.

3 Combine the beer and the coffee (we use James's freshly roasted coffee) in a bowl, working as quickly as you can, dunk half of the sponge finger into the mixture and arrange in a tight layer over the cream.

4 Spread the second third of the cream mixture, repeat with the last sponge fingers and the rest of the cream mixture.

5 Grate chocolate (we use a mixture of Sue Gilmour's Botanicals Rose Chocolate and her Venezuelan Dark Chocolate) over the top of the tiramisu. Leave to set in the fridge over night... or as long as you can wait without sticking your finger in for a sneaky try!

Did you know… the ancient Babylonians were the first to brew – they took their beer so seriously that if you brewed a bad batch it was your punishment to be drowned in it!

Serves: 6-8
- 6 large egg yolks, room temp
- 125g (4½oz) sugar
- 450g (1lb) mascarpone cheese
- 4 large egg whites
- 2 teaspoons Forage Fine Foods rose petal preserve
- 2 packets ladyfingers
- 350ml Mayfields stout
- 1 double espresso
- Rose flavoured chocolate, for grating

hops

Just Rachel

"For centuries, iced desserts were a luxury and the origins of ice cream are shrouded in mystery. Some sources claim that the Roman Emperor Nero sent his slaves into the mountains to fetch snow to mix with nectar, fruit pulp, and honey in about 50 AD. Other sources credit the Chinese with inventing ice cream: the Chinese emperor T'ang of Shang (618 -907 AD) kept 94 'ice men' at his palace to collect ice so that he could eat a frozen mixture of fermented milk, flour and camphor. At Just Rachel we use rather more palatable ingredients: thick Herefordshire cream, British sugar, local fruits and the best ingredients from around the world to make our award-winning products for your delectation." **Rachel, Just Rachel**

Caramelised Apple and Salted Caramel Ice Cream Tarts

1 To make the caramel sauce, weigh the white sugar into a large heavy bottomed pan and heat gently, shaking the pan occasionally until the sugar starts to turn golden brown and syrupy. Heat the whipping cream in a pan on the stove or in a large measuring jug in the microwave until just bubbling (do not let it boil over) then pour onto the syrupy sugar, stirring vigorously. Be careful because it will boil up and it is VERY hot! Stir until smooth then cook for 5 mins until a lovely rich golden brown colour. Leave to cool.

2 To prepare the apples, peel and core the apples and slice into segments. Heat the butter in a large frying pan until bubbling gently. Stir in the sugar, then add the apples and keep stirring gently until they are softened and well coated in the buttery-sugary mix. Leave to cool.

3 Just before you want to eat the dessert… place two shortcrust cases on each dish, spoon a generous amount of caramel into the cases. Spread the apple slices over the caramel and scoop a ball of ice cream on top of the apples. Drizzle any remaining caramel sauce over the ice cream and serve at once.

All the elements of this dessert can be prepared well in advance. It just needs a few mins to assemble it when you are ready to serve it.

Serves: **4**

For the caramel sauce:
- 125g (4½oz) granulated sugar
- 250ml (9oz) Herefordshire whipping cream

For the caramelised apples:
- 2 large Herefordshire eating apples
- 125g (4½oz) butter
- 125g (4½oz) soft brown sugar

- 8 individual ready-cooked sweet shortcrust tart cases (or you can make your own if you have time!)
- 500ml tub of Just Rachel Salted Caramel Ice Cream

Bulmers Cider

"In 1887, Fred and Percy Bulmer used apples from Rectory Orchard Credenhill, where their father was rector to make their first ciders. Their father, the reverend Charles Bulmer, was an enthusiastic horticulturist and a keen amateur cider maker, but it was his wife's advice that persuaded the 20 year-old son to devote his energies to the drinks market. 'Food and drink never go out of fashion,' she said wisely. The business has progressed and expanded over the 20th century and into the 21st becoming the largest apple pressing mill in the world. In 1888 Percy Bulmer arranged to buy enough apples from the local farmers to produce 4000 gallons of cider – still today most of the apples are provided by local farmers, who maintain the beautiful orchards that form part of the patchwork of Herefordshire's rich landscape."

Spiced Cider Sorbet

Serves: 6
- 568ml (1 pint) Bulmers Cider
- 100g (3½oz) sugar
- 100ml (3½fl oz) water
- 1 cinnamon stick, broken
- 4 cloves
- 4 allspice berries
- 1 pinch ground nutmeg
- ½ teaspoon grated ginger
- Peel of ½ orange

1 Add the sugar and water to a pan and bring to the boil to dissolve the sugar and make a syrup, then add all the spices and orange peel.

2 Turn down the heat, pour the cider into the pan, and heat gently. Be careful not to boil the mixture as you will boil off the alcohol (unless of course you want to make a less alcoholic version). Allow to cool, strain out the spices and then chill down in the fridge for a few hours (or overnight).

3 Pour the mixture into an ice cream maker (follow your ice cream makers instructions, as they do vary depending on the model), alternatively pour into a freezable container, and pop in the freezer, making sure to go back to your sorbet to agitate regularly as the mixture freezes. The sorbet can be served as soon as it has frozen to a fluffy, spoonable consistency, or you can leave it in your freezer longer if you prefer a firmer sorbet.

Upper Newton Farmhouse (Kinnersley Cottages)

"Everything with us is slow – slow growing vegetables, slow food, slow felting, slow dyeing, slow gardening, slow cooking and slow holidays. Our 'slow' means care and time taken to help guests really unwind and enjoy the farm and countryside. We have planted a colourful and fragrant, bee-friendly herb garden – gorgeous for the inhabitants of the bee hives and guests alike. Cyclists and walkers are particularly welcome at Upper Newton, and in case it is wet we are totally geared up to dry clothes and shoes and wash down bicycles, we also run courses on felt making and dyeing. All is comfortable here – even our birds have felted fleece birdhouses!" **Pearl Taylor**

Newton Farmhouse Honey and Lavender Shortbread Biscuits

1 Beat the butter and sugar and essence until creamy consistency, work in the flours, honey, rind and flowers (you will need to experiment with your own honey to get the right sweetness).

2 Press the mixture into a greased tin, either shaped (like mine) or into a loose-based cake tin. Sprinkle with sugar and bake at 160°C (320°F, Gas Mark 3) for 30-35 mins.

3 Watch carefully in the last few mins – you need a light golden brown. Remove from the oven. If in a flat tin, mark out your portions, leave to cool and then remove carefully from the mould or base.

I like to grate a little more lemon rind on prior to serving as it cuts through the sweetness and seems to enhance the lavender flavour.

Makes: 20 biscuits
- 100g (3½oz) soft unsalted butter
- 100g (3½oz) plain flour
- 60g (2½oz) rice flour
- Grated rind of two small lemons
- 8 drops hot lavender essence
- 1 teaspoon Herefordshire honey
- 1 pinch of fresh (or dried) lavender flowers
- A little lavender sugar to sprinkle before baking

honey bee

Mycocoa

"I stumbled into becoming a chocolatier. Whilst living in Brighton I was lucky enough to get a job at Choccywoccydoodah, where I trained and worked for several years. Then my husband and I packed up and travelled the world, where I sampled all sorts of unusual chocolate horrors and delicacies. On our return we moved to Somerset where I worked for another local chocolate company, but I was born and raised in Herefordshire, so having children drew us back to the county. I wanted to use my chocolate skills to create beautiful, delicious treats, so Mycocoa was born. I love playing with flavours, but the look and design of my chocolate is very important. I love people to see my bars and I love how excited they get when trying to choose a flavour. A feast for the eyes as well as the belly! Herefordians certainly enjoy their chocolate!" **Ray Farr**

Makes: 25-30
- 125ml (4½fl oz) local ale
- 350g (12oz) milk chocolate
- 25g (1oz) muscavado sugar
- Extra chocolate of your choice for dipping/drizzling the truffles

Local Ale Truffles

1 Put ¼ of the ale (I used Wye Valley Butty Bach) and the sugar in a saucepan and stir over low heat until the sugar is fully dissolved. Add the remaining ale and warm until you can see the alcohol's vapours being released from the surface. The ale needs only be warm enough to melt the chocolate – overheating it will cook off the alcohol.

2 Add the chocolate gradually and keep stirring until smooth. Cool in the fridge for minimum of 1 hour (24 hours is good). If your truffle mix is still very soft and not at a consistency where you could roll it into a ball with your hands, add some more melted chocolate to help firm up the mixture. Then either pipe into prepared chocolate shells, or hand roll into little balls.

3 Use chocolate for coating. You could coat them in white, dark or milk chocolate. Dip each truffle into melted chocolate (or even roll them in a mixture of icing sugar and cocoa) Then allow to set. A decoration of drizzled chocolate in an alternate colour looks good on these truffles, eg. dark choc coated truffles drizzled in white choc.

Hereford Cathedral School

"Hereford Cathedral School has great history and is one of the UK's leading independent co-educational day schools. Part of the Hereford Cathedral Foundation, dating back to 676, it stands as one of the oldest schools still in existence and has a strong tradition of providing an outstanding educational experience. Floreat Schola Herefordensis! As the Catering Manager at the school, my catering department is exceptionally busy with at least 700 hungry pupils and staff to serve every lunchtime (much of what we serve is locally procured, including the milk, meat and vegetables) but alongside this we are busy supplying sports teas, packed lunches, buffet lunches, VIP canapé receptions, summer ball catering and networking dinners. Being at the heart of Hereford, we also love getting involved with the Flavours of Herefordshire Festival, where we run a café and a homemade gourmet beef burger stand." **Andy Boast**

Andy's Herefordshire Apple Teabread

1 Make a strong tea using the teabags and boiling water. Remove the teabags and pour over the fruit, sugar, apple juice and mixed spice, stir and leave to stew overnight.

2 The following day, add the flour, egg and apple and mix well.

3 Tip into a greased 900g (2lb) loaf tin, and cook at 150°C (300°F, Gas Mark 2) for 2 hours.

Serves: 20 hungry children
- 225g (8oz) dried mixed fruit
- 225g (8oz) light muscavado Sugar
- 150ml (¼ pint) boiling water
- 1 normal teabag
- 1 apple and cinnamon teabag
- 150ml (¼ pint) local apple juice (or cider!)
- ½ teaspoon mixed spice
- 275g (10oz) self raising flour
- 1 egg
- 1 apple, grated

The Courtyard Café Bar

"I was inspired to cook by my mother – she's ninety this year and she still likes to experiment! Back in 2006 I just baked a few cakes for our customers. Now as Catering Manager at The Courtyard I lead a small team, passionate about producing both traditional and imaginative new dishes, prepared using quality local ingredients. I still like baking best – bread, quiches, pastry and homely recipes, my favourite being cheese scones. I am always developing and inventing: I'm having a gluten free push at the moment and the cakes are going down a storm. Just what you need before settling into your seat for a Christmas pantomime, a serious film or an evening of live comedy." **Jan Pitts**

Serves: 8
For the cake:
- 200g (7oz) butter, softened
- 200g (7oz) golden caster sugar
- 4 eggs (Country Flavours Free Range)
- 175g (6oz) ground almonds
- 250g (9oz) mashed potatoes (made without salt)
- Zest of 3 lemons
- 2 teaspoons gluten-free baking powder

For the drizzle:
- 4 tablespoons granulated sugar
- Juice of 1 lemon

For the lemon curd:
- Juice and zest 4 medium lemons
- 250g (9oz) butter
- 450g (1lb) caster sugar
- 5 eggs beaten

Gluten Free Lemon Drizzle Cake

1 Heat oven to 180°C (350°F, Gas Mark 4). Butter and line a deep, 20cm (8 inch) round cake tin. Beat the sugar and butter together until light and fluffy, then gradually add the eggs (we used Country Flavours Free Range) one at a time, beating after each addition. Fold in the almonds, cold mashed potato (we used Green Farm Potatoes), lemon zest and baking powder.

2 Tip the mixture into the tin, level the top, then bake for 40-45 mins or until golden and a skewer inserted into the middle of the cake comes out clean. Turn out onto a wire rack after 10 mins cooling.

3 Mix the granulated sugar and the lemon juice together, then spoon over the top of the cake, letting it drip down the sides. Let the cake cool completely before slicing.

4 For the lemon curd, place the juice and lemon zest in a bowl on top of a saucepan of boiling water. Add the butter and caster sugar and stir gently over a low heat until the sugar is completely dissolved.

5 Take the pan from the heat and strain in the beaten eggs. Put back on a low heat and cook gently until the mixture coats the back of the spoon, stirring occasionally. This curd can be kept in the fridge for up to 4 weeks. (But I guarantee it will be eaten much sooner!).

Slice the cake; serve with a generous dollop of the lemon curd, some Bartonsham Farm whipped cream and some local raspberries. Enjoy!

This cake can also be made nut-free by substituting polenta for the ground almonds.

Castle Brook Vineyard

"Our vineyards are ideally located on sunny south-facing slopes of an ancient meander valley of the River Wye which were originally terraced and planted by the Romans. Castle Brook vineyard was re-established by the Chinn family in 2004 to produce the finest sparkling wines. We use the classic fizz varieties of Chardonnay, Pinot Noir and Pinot Meunier, and the traditional methods developed by monks in 17th century England, now time-honoured by a certain French region! Chinn-Chinn has a deliciously delicate, crisp palate with a hint of lemon blossom. Brioche and toasty yeast notes add complexity to the finish."
Chris Chinn

Serves: **6**

For the jelly:
- 7 gelatine leaves
- 300g (11oz) caster sugar
- 200ml (7fl oz) water
- Zest and juice of 2 lemons
- 500ml (17½fl oz) Chinn-Chinn sparkling wine
- 200g fresh blueberries

For the frosted decorations:
- 200g (7oz) fresh blueberries
- 4 roses
- 1 egg white
- 4 tablespoons vanilla sugar

Chinn-Chinn Sparkling Wine and Blueberry Jelly

1 Pop your jelly moulds into the fridge to chill. Soak the gelatine leaves in cold water to soften.

2 In a saucepan, dissolve the sugar in 100ml (3½fl oz) water with the lemon zest, and simmer gently for 5 mins. Remove from the heat and add the lemon juice. Drain the gelatine leaves and stir into the hot syrup to dissolve. Leave to cool for 10 mins, then add the sparkling wine.

3 Pour half the mixture into the chilled moulds and refrigerate for 3 hours. Scatter over the blueberries and add the rest of the jelly. Return to the fridge for 6 hours to set completely.

4 To make the frosted blueberries and rose petals, first wash and dry the fruit and petals. Lightly whisk the egg white and add the blueberries and petals, then drain in a sieve. Roll the coated berries in the sugar, spread on a lined tray and leave at room temperature to dry. Don't refrigerate or the sugar will dissolve.

When ready to serve, turn out your jelly and decorate with the frosted berries and petals, and if this all sounds like too much work, Chinn-Chinn is great drunk chilled with a couple of blueberries dropped in...simple!

The Lion, Leintwardine

"Since we bought the Lion two years ago we have enjoyed the building and refurbishment of a wonderful old pub. We specialise in modern British cuisine, freshly cooked, using local produce. The lamb for instance, comes from our own farm, summer peas and beans are collected from a local farm and delivered to The Lion within hours of being picked and our eggs are in the kitchens on the day they were laid. However, one of the things that I have enjoyed most about having my own pub is having a venue for my band 'The Chiefs' (a group of locals) to play our gigs whenever we feel like it, rocking here, on the banks of the River Teme." **William Watkins**

Glazed Lemon Tart with Mascarpone and Elderflower Ice Cream

1 First of all make the ice cream. Beat the egg yolks and sugar together and put to one side. Heat the milk making sure it doesn't come to the boil. Add the hot milk to the eggs and sugar and leave to cool. When chilled beat in the mascarpone and the elderflower cordial and churn in an ice cream maker until thick (if you do not have an ice cream maker put the mixture in the freezer and stir regularly until frozen).

2 For the pastry, mix together the butter and sieved flour until breadcrumb consistency, add the icing sugar and fold in the egg yolks. Add the water little by little to create a smooth pliable pastry. Cling film the mix and leave to rest for a couple of hours.

3 Once rested, roll the pastry out and line a shallow tart case or flan tin. Bake with baking beans at 200°C (400°F, Gas Mark 6) for 15 mins. Remove the baking beans, reduce the temperature to 180°C (350°F, Gas Mark 4), bake for a further 10 mins, until golden.

4 For the filling, beat the eggs and egg whites together. Sift the icing sugar into a bowl, then gradually beat in the eggs until smooth. Stir in the lemon zest and the juice. Beat the crème fraîche in a medium bowl until smooth, then slowly stir in the lemon mix until well blended. Transfer to a jug, and pour two thirds into the warm pastry case. Place in the oven with the oven shelf half out, pour in the rest of the filling. Reduce the heat to 150°C (300°F, Gas Mark 2). Bake for 25-30 mins until barely set with a slight wobble in the middle. Cool for about 1 hour.

5 Glaze. Slice a portion, sprinkle with a light dusting of caster sugar and brown with a blowtorch until crystallised and golden brown.

We serve our tart and ice cream with a garnish of cubed fruits, micro herbs, lemon zest and coulis.

Serves: 8-10

For the pastry:
- 120g (4½oz) unsalted butter, at room temperature, diced
- 75g (3oz) icing sugar, sieved
- 3 large egg yolks, beaten
- 250g (9oz) plain flour, sieved
- 2 tablespoons water

For the tart filling:
- 3 large eggs,
- 2 medium egg whites
- 140g (4¾oz) icing sugar, plus extra for dusting
- 2 tablespoons finely grated lemon zest (about 4 lemons)
- 125ml (4½fl oz) lemon juice, approx. 4-5 lemons
- 200ml (7fl oz) crème fraîche
- Caster sugar, to glaze

For the ice cream:
- 150g (5oz) mascarpone
- 75ml (3fl oz) milk
- 3 egg yolks
- 2oz caster sugar
- 35ml (1¼fl oz) elderflower cordial

Rowlestone Farmhouse Ice Cream

"Our family has farmed here for three generations, which is eighty years. Our 'open farm' venture started in 2007 has allowed us to share this idyllic setting both with campers and the visiting general public alike. Whether taking the circular walk from the cafe through the wildlife garden, copses, ancient woodlands and wildflower meadow, affording spectacular views of this borders area en-route and a glimpse of history at the lime kilns; or whether burning off some energy on the woodland adventure trail, a smooth ice cream or sundae from the farm's parlour is a just reward for an afternoon's exertion!"
Mary and Mark Williams

Rowlestone Hot Raspberry Sundae

Serves: 4
- 8 large scoops Rowlestone Court Vanilla Madagaskar Ice Cream
- 300g raspberries
- 1 tablespoon caster sugar
- 200ml double cream
- 100g mini marshmallows
- 400g meringue nests (or homemade meringue)

1 Warm the raspberries and sugar gently in a pan, crushing some of them slightly, reserving four of the raspberries for the decoration. Whip the cream (we use a cream whipper here, but you can get the same result at home by hand whipping and then piping your cream). Crush the meringue.

2 In a tall sundae glass, layer the warmed raspberries, mini marshmallows, meringue, then the ice cream, and repeat. Finish with a piping of the cream, and a raspberry on the top!

Windmill Hill Fruits

"Luckily for us Herefordshire has one of the best climates and topography for fruit production! We have been farming at our family farm, Windmill Hill near Ross, for three generations, developing different techniques for the best production of our classic, award-winning, British summer fruits. It is also important to us that we continue to educate as many youngsters about our food and where it comes from which is why we take part in open farm days and farm educational programmes too. Not many people would know that Herefordshire grows around 30% of the British blackcurrant crop, nor that raspberries and strawberries are members of the rose family, or that strawberries are the only fruit with their seeds on the outside!" **Anthony and Christine Snell**

Berry Best Summerfruit Pavlova

Serves: 6-8
- 4 egg whites
- 225g (8oz) caster sugar
- 1 teaspoon white wine vinegar
- 1 teaspoon cornflour
- 300ml (11fl oz) whipping cream
- 1 packet Windmill Hill British Summer Fruits

1 Heat the oven to 170°C (325°F, Gas Mark 3) and lay some baking parchment (or a silicon sheet) on a baking tray.

2 Whisk the egg whites in a large bowl, until they form stiff shiny peaks. Then whisk in the sugar, a little at a time. Once all the sugar is added continue to whisk for a few mins. Your meringue should be glossy and stand up in peaks. Finally whisk in the cornflour and vinegar.

3 Make a 20cm (8 inch) circle of the meringue on your baking sheet, then spoon even dollops around the edge, lifting the spoon with a flourish to give a peak in the centre of each dollop.

4 Pop in the oven, and immediately turn the oven down to 110°C (225°F, Gas Mark ¼). Leave for 1-1½ hours or until a very slight golden colour appears on the meringue. Turn your oven off and leave the meringue to cool in the oven. This will make sure your meringue has dried out well (you can even do this the night before and leave it in the cold oven overnight).

5 When ready to serve, whip up the whipping cream, and spoon into the centre of the pavlova. Arrange your Windmill Hill British Summer Fruits over the top of the cream and finish with a sprig of mint.

A gorgeous, and very easy, show stopper dessert!

Jus Single Variety Apple Juice

"At Jus we grow most of the apples used in our single variety apple juice on our farm, and those we can't are sourced from other Herefordshire farmers. They are picked only when ripe and ready in the autumn. Each individual variety is pressed and pasteurised to capture the natural flavour and sweetness of the apple to make our Jus. Some of the varieties we produce are Bramley's Seedling, Cox's Orange Pippin, Discovery, Katy, Lord Lambourne, Elstar, Worcester Pearmain and Egremont Russet. The different types of apples all have different flavours and sweetness, ranging from dry (like the Bramley's Seedling), medium (like the Lord Lambourne) to sweet (like the Egremont Russet)." **Jane Skittery**

Fresh Fruit Salad

Serves: 4
- 1 eating apple
- 1 orange
- 50g (2oz) grapes
- ⅓ melon
- 50g (2oz) strawberries
- Juice of 1 lemon
- 250ml (9fl oz) Jus Single Variety Apple Juice

1 Put the apple juice and lemon juice into a bowl. Quarter the apple and remove the core, then slice the quarters into two or three slices and add to the bowl.

2 Cut the melon from the skin and cut into bite size chunks (or if you have a melon baller, make some melon balls) and add to bowl.

3 Peel and cut the orange into segments, cut the grapes in half and remove any pips, cut the strawberries either into half or quarter depending on the size, and add them all to the bowl.

4 Carefully and gently mix the fruit up and refrigerate to chill before serving. Garnish with a mint sprig.

You can add or change the fruits to the fruits you like to eat. The apple juice can be any variety to suit your taste, as the fruit is sweet. We used Cox's Orange Pippin (a lovely medium) apple juice, to go with the Cox's Orange Pippin apple.

apple

Noke Lane Bakery

"I've just completed a 10 month bakery course at the School of Artisan Food in Nottinghamshire. My adopted home county of Herefordshire is where my heart is and where I will be setting up a small artisan bakery opening in Spring 2014 (small orders welcome before)! Whilst my training is primarily bread I've had the opportunity to develop some pâtisserie skills and learn some tips and tricks from leading pâtissiers. This especially helped with my macaron making obsession. My base recipe is inspired by Jill Colonna's great book 'Mad about Macarons' which I've adapted to reflect what I've learnt from others. I made these for my final exams, including making the fondant snails as a bit of fun." **Tory Dickinson**

Apple and Blackberry Macarons

1 Line 2 baking sheets with non-stick baking paper. Make a reusable template sheet that can be slid under the baking paper when piping out, by drawing 4cm (1½ inch) circles with a dark pen, keeping each circle about 6cm (2½ inches) apart. Tip – a small jar lid is ideal to draw around. You'll probably get about 20 circles on one sheet. Scald the mixing bowl for the meringue, by rinsing in boiling water and if needed mop up any water left with a clean cloth. Preheat oven to 160°C, (320°F, Gas Mark 3).

2 Sieve the almonds to remove large or coarse pieces before weighing out. Then add to the icing sugar and lightly hand whisk to combine evenly. In a separate bowl, whisk egg whites to soft peaks and then start to add the caster sugar by tablespoons until get you glossy firm peaks. Add food colouring and give final whisk to set colour. Take about a third of the meringue and mix vigorously into almond/icing sugar mix. Its best to use a spatula. Ensure all of the dry ingredients are blended well. Add the next third and again mix vigorously. The mixture will start to loosen up considerably. Add the final third mixing in more gently until fully combined. When the spatula is lifted out of the mix it should run slowly back into the bowl in a ribbon.

3 Put in piping bag with 1cm (½ inch) size piping nozzle. Its best to pipe a mix this size in a couple of batches. Pipe out the discs to the template size. Leave to sit for approx. 30 mins to skin over as this helps to produce the distinct 'feet' they have.

4 Bake one tray at a time for 12-13 mins in middle of oven. To check if baked gently touch top of macaron and if there is still a wobble it'll need a couple more mins. Remove from the oven and transfer to cooling racks to fully cool before removing from the baking paper.

5 For the apple curd buttercream, cream the butter then incorporate the apple curd. The consistency should be loose enough to pipe but not run.

6 Sort out macarons into pairs (aiming to get best size match). Line them up with one row flat side up and the other flat side down. Pipe the apple curd butter cream onto flat side up macarons using a star shaped 1cm (½ inch) piping nozzle. Then gently put the two shells together with a slight circular motion to evenly squash and distribute the filling. For the jelly filling, I set mine onto a baking sheet, then cut out discs for a neat finish.

Macarons can be kept in the fridge for 24 hours or frozen for up to a month, but I'm sure they'll get eaten before that!

Makes: **18 pairs**

For the macarons:
- 150g (5oz) egg whites, approx. 4
- 100g (3½oz) white caster sugar
- 180g (6¼oz) ground almonds
- 270g (9½oz) icing sugar, sifted
- A few drops food colouring

For the apple curd buttercream:
- 100g (3½oz) butter
- 120g (4¼oz) apple curd

- Blackberry jelly (or jam)

Tip – I use up the egg yolks to make curds, custard or mayonnaise.

Shepherds Ice Cream

"When we started Shepherds Ice Cream in 1987, we were the first people to make ice cream from sheep's milk in the UK! Most people did not realise that sheep, like cows, are divided into two different strains – those bred for meat and those bred for milk. Historically, we have been milking sheep for much longer than we have been milking cows; think about the sheep in the Bible – they were kept primarily for milk. And of course the occasional lamb would be slaughtered on special feast days!" **Juliet Noble**

Shepherds Ice Cream Sundae

1 For the coulis, simply combine the raspberries, icing sugar and Framboise in a blender, until smooth, then pass through a fine sieve.

2 For the crème chantilly, split the vanilla pod, scrape out the seeds and add with the sugar, to the cream in a large bowl whisk to soft peaks.

3 Assemble the sundae, here you can have fun and add the elements in whatever order you fancy. We started with a dollop of crème chantilly, then a scoop of chocolate ice cream, then the raspberry sorbet, then the vanilla ice cream, finishing with a good dollop of the crème chantilly, and a drizzle of the coulis. Fill any gaps with the raspberries. Top with the nuts, chocolate shavings, and finish with wafer and a mint sprig.

Sundaes are a great treat for adults and children alike. Kids love to get creative and add their own toppings (why not try a homemade chocolate sauce – melt some chocolate with a little cream and hot water), or why not try an adult version and spike the crème chantilly with a little brandy.

Serves: 4
- 1 tub Shepherds Vanilla Sheep's Milk Ice Cream
- 1 tub Shepherds Chocolate Sheep's Milk Ice Cream
- 1 tub Shepherds Raspberry Sorbet

- 1 sprinkle chopped nuts
- 1 sprinkle chocolate shavings
- 1 handful raspberries
- 4 mint sprigs
- 4 wafers

For the raspberry coulis:
- 300g (10½oz) raspberries
- 1-2 tablespoons icing sugar
- 1 tablespoon Jo Hilditch Framboise

For the crème chantilly:
- 300ml (10½fl oz) double cream
- 1-2 tablespoons icing sugar
- 1 vanilla pod

Wye Valley Granola

"Wye Valley Granola is a delicious healthy artisan cereal made of oats, seeds and nuts, baked by hand in a blend of maple and carob fruit syrup, Herefordshire apple juice and just a touch of golden rapeseed oil (from Herefordshire of course!). We use nothing but the finest ingredients which are local where possible, and sourced only from responsible, quality and traceable sources. I'm passionate about my food – one of the best things about living in Herefordshire, is that I am surrounded by fabulous delis, farm shops and farmer's markets, where people, like me, really do care about what goes into their food. So when I struggled to find a granola that wasn't full of refined sugars and processed fats, I set about making my own using only the finest local Herefordshire ingredients." **Angharad Warren**

Wye Valley Granola Breakfast Sundae

1 Crush the strawberries with a fork in a bowl, and for those who prefer things a touch sweeter, blend in a teaspoon of coconut palm sugar (a healthier, unrefined sweetener made from the nectar of coconut palm blossoms).

2 Spoon the strawberry mixture into a sundae glass and cover with a layer of yoghurt followed by a layer of granola.

3 Repeat this process until the ingredients are used up and top with a sprinkling of fresh blueberries.

Serves: 1
- 50g (2oz) of Wye Valley Granola
- 12 small strawberries
- Small handful of blueberries
- Small tub of creamy natural yoghurt
- 1 sprinkle of coconut palm sugar (available at all good health shops)

strawberry

Hedonist Bakery

"My farming career brought us to Herefordshire. In 2004 I moved from growing the grain to selling the bread by starting a frozen bakery wholesale business. Having gained knowledge of traditional craft bakery techniques and recipes over the following couple of years, I left this wholesale business behind to create a unique range of the finest handmade additive free breads. We are innovative in only part-baking our breads, so you can finish the baking off at home, anytime of the day, with all the enjoyment of the aroma and taste of freshly baked bread. Although we are proud to supply nationally we remain firmly attached to our Herefordshire roots, and of course to Ross-on-Wye." **Steven Mackintosh**

Serves: 2
- 4 slices of Hedonist Bakery Raisin and Cobnut Bread
- 3 free range eggs
- 185ml (6½fl oz) milk
- 250g (9oz) fresh (or frozen defrosted) berries
- 60g (2½oz) caster sugar
- ½ lemon, juiced
- 30g (1¼oz) salted butter
- 25g (1oz) icing sugar

Hedonist's Eggy Toast with Berry Sauce

1 Place most of the berries (we used Windmill Hill Summer Berries), caster sugar and lemon juice in a blender and blend until nearly smooth. Reserve a few berries to add to the sauce after blending. Set the sauce to one side.

2 Beat the eggs and the milk together. Take the slices of Hedonist Raisin and Cobnut Bread and soak in the egg mixture.

3 In a non-stick frying pan melt the butter until sizzling and add the slices of bread. Fry on a medium heat and flip bread over when golden brown. When both sides are golden, place slices on a serving plate and top with the berry sauce. Dust with icing sugar to finish.

This is a great recipe to use up any forgotten bread that may be a few days old. But, by using our Raisin and Cobnut loaf, which contains honey and rosemary it turns this simple recipe into a delicious and healthy breakfast treat.

Cool cocktails
and refreshing drinks

The Great British Florist

"We are based at Wiggly Wigglers in Blakemere – we're busy bunnies here, helping lead a British Flower revolution! At the moment just 10% of the flowers sold in the UK are actually grown here, and to us (and many others), this is just a little tinsy bit raving mad. Our project is to get all consumers to commit to only British Flowers. Because our flowers are 'Grown not Flown', they have a fraction of the average flower miles, and since they don't have to travel as far, they look gorgeous and stay fresh and scented for longer, it is also brilliant for our biodiversity. Some of them even taste good too! The humble English rose being a prime example." **Heather Gorringe**

Serves: **2**

- 4 rose flowers
- 200g (7oz) sugar
- 100ml (4fl oz) water
- ½ lemon, zest and juice
- 1 sprig lemon balm
- 1 sprig mint
- 1 head lavender
- 1 small sprig rosemary
- 75ml (3fl oz) Chase Vodka
- 275ml (½ pint) sparkling water

Great British Flowery Fizz

1 To make the ice cubes, take some rose petals (the smaller inside ones work best) and add to an ice tray, fill the tray half way with water and place into the freezer. Once the first half has frozen, top up with more water, and return to the freezer to encase the petals in the ice.

2 To make the rose syrup, pull the petals from the rose heads, rinse and add to a small saucepan with the sugar and water, simmer until the mixture has thickened into a syrup. Add 1 drop of natural food colouring, if you desire. Strain through a sieve and pour into hot sterilised bottle to store. The syrup will keep for two weeks in the refrigerator (the petals can also be cooled on a silicon baking sheet to add as a sweet and sticky topping to desserts like ice cream).

3 For the cocktail, pour the vodka into a cocktail shaker with some ice. Add the lemon zest and a squeeze of the juice, the lemon balm, mint, a couple of lavender petals and rosemary sprig, and shake well.

4 Add the petal ice cubes to highball glasses. Pour the shaken vodka through a sieve into the glasses. Add a drizzle of the rose syrup and gently top up the drink with fizzy water.

Sit back, relax and enjoy, whilst our beautiful edible bouquet fills your room with its wonderful scent.

Celtic Vale Natural Mineral Water

"We established Celtic Vale in the early 80's as a diversification from sheep farming. After reading an article in 'Farmers Weekly' about increasing demand for bottled water, my dad, Glyn, decided to get the spring on our farm tested. And what a dramatic effect this had on the direction of our family business! The spring was pure, stable in mineral content and prolific (up to 80,000 gallons a day). It easily met the high standards needed to be designated as one of the UK's recognised Mineral Water Sources. The Celtic Vale Spring rises under natural pressure, surfacing at 800 feet above sea level, high above any farm land which greatly contributes to its exceptional purity and low nitrate content. Everyone knows water is vital to our existence, it's recommended we need 1.2 litres per day. There are many ways to enjoy water and most recipes can be vastly improved by using natural water as an ingredient!" **Melanie Watkins**

Makes: approx. 750ml (1¼ pints)
- 1.5kg (3lbs 5oz) rhubarb, roughly chopped
- 1 vanilla pod
- 750ml (1¼ pints) Celtic Vale Natural Mineral Water, Still
- Caster sugar
- Lemon juice

Rhubarb and Vanilla Pod Cordial

1 Place the Celtic Vale Mineral Water, rhubarb and split vanilla pod into a pan and cook slowly over a low heat until the juices start to flow, then turn up the heat a little and cook until the rhubarb is soft.

2 Line a large bowl with muslin and tip in the mixture, pull the corners together, tie and strain off the liquid.

3 Measure the juice: for every litre add 750g (1lb 10oz) of sugar and 75ml (3fl oz) lemon juice. Pour into a pan and gently heat until the sugar dissolves (do not boil). Pour into sterilised bottles and seal.

This makes a fabulous non alcoholic summer drink (serve 1 part cordial with 3 parts Celtic Vale still or sparkling water over ice), but is also delicious if used in a cocktail with our sparkling water and gin or vodka.

...rhubarb

British Cassis

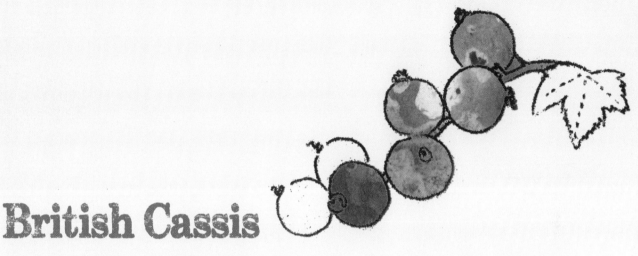

"My great grandfather used to sell his blackcurrants in the local wholesale markets, branding his Herefordshire berries as the best. Our berries are still brill, grown on the rolling hills of our farm near the Welsh border. And who would have known as I sipped a Kir Royale aged 16 on my French exchange in champagne country, wondering why my Dad didn't turn his blackcurrants into a cocktail drink, that nearly 40 years later I would have been making our own British version of that French staple. During the 80 years that we have been growing this healthy black berry, we have grown for jam, for the local fruit market, for that famous British drink, and now for our own Cassis. One might say it's been a long and fruitful journey!" **Jo Hilditch**

Berry Bomb

1 In a 35ml shot glass pour the Cassis, cointreau and rum for a warming, fruity shot on a crisp cold winter's day!

I drink mine slightly warmed.

Serves: 1
- 17ml Cassis
- 10ml Cointreau
- 7ml Rum

The Shack Revolution

"My brother and I have been making our own apple juice for a number of years now, under the brand Mannings Juice, using the fruit from our family fruit farm. We were after something a bit more exciting so we began to travel the UK making our fresh juices and cocktails at events, food festivals, weddings and parties, which was very exciting! The first 'Juice Shack' was made from old apple boxes and was so popular we named the business 'The Shack Revolution'! We believe in keeping things fun, fresh and British, so why not have a crack at our juicy cocktails yourself, they are all very easy to make. We hope you enjoy!" **James and Richard Manning**

The Shack's Juicy Trio

Apple and Raspberry Mojito

Simply place all 5 ingredients into the blender (including the alcohol) and whizz away! Top tip – do not leave the blender going by itself, instead keep tapping the pulse button until you can see the raspberries and mint breaking up. You do not want to blitz the whole thing, it will become very frothy and you will lose the juice!

Apple, Carrot and Ginger

Blend the apple juice and the ginger (make sure you take the skin off) at full power for around 10 seconds to break up the ginger. Run the carrots through the juicer, and pour the juice into the blender along with the ice cubes, give the blender one last blast to mix up all the ingredients. Top tip – if you like ginger then add more. This one goes great with gin.

Orchard Lemonade

Half the lemon is the average, but to make it sharper add the whole lemon. Simply squeeze the lemon juice into the blender along with the apple juice and ice cubes. Whizz the blender for 5 seconds and you're done! This is a really healthy alternative to traditional lemonade and can be kept in your fridge for up to a week because the lemon will naturally preserve the apple juice! Top tip – why not add a few strawberries or raspberries into the blender to make a fruity lemonade, or simply add some vodka to make it into a zingy cocktail!

Makes: 1 of each

For the apple and raspberry mojito:
- 220ml (8fl oz) apple juice
- 1 shot white rum
- 6 raspberries (fresh or frozen)
- 6-8 leaves of mint
- 4 ice cubes (optional)

For the apple, carrot and ginger:
- 220ml (8fl oz) apple juice
- 2 carrots
- Ginger (1 sugar cube size amount)
- 4 ice cubes (optional)

For the orchard lemonade:
- 1 lemon
- 250ml (9fl oz) apple juice
- 4 ice cubes

(No sugar or water needed)

Lulham Court Vineyard

"Although we are only small, we are beautiful! Originally planted in 1979 as part of our farm diversity policy, we have three acres of Muller Thurgau, Reichensteiner and Syval Blanc vines. I'm told I have green fingers, but mostly they are just quite dirty brown! I take great care in producing my wine and critics have found my Reichensteiner 'deliciously crisp, with a slightly floral nose'! I think it makes an ideal aperitif, or lunchtime accompaniment to fish in particular – as do my friends and family – there seems to be no holding back!" **Phil Pennington**

Serves: 8
- 1 bottle of Lulham Court Sparkling Wine, chilled
- 300ml (10½fl oz) local apple juice
- 200ml (7fl oz) Jo Hilditch Fraise
- 100g (3½oz) local strawberries
- 1 Herefordshire apple
- 1 tablespoon caster sugar
- 1 sprig of thyme
- ½ lemon, sliced
- 1 splash of lemon juice (to taste)

Summer Vineyard Glow

1 Quarter the strawberries. Core and slice the apple. Remove the thyme leaves from the sprig and roughly chop. Place the fruit and thyme in a large punch bowl with a little lemon juice, and the sugar, stir to coat the fruit.

2 Add the Jo Hilditch Fraise and the apple juice, then gently pour in the Lulham Court Sparkling Wine. Add the lemon slices and a little splash more lemon if needed. Chill in the fridge.

Enjoy served with ice, on a warm summer's afternoon, with friends.

lemon

Watercress Harrys

"When a chef heads to market they are looking for the best produce to create the perfect dish. As a mixologist (a bar chef!), being in a county like Herefordshire I am surrounded by amazing products to help me create fantastic cocktails and mocktails. The intense flavours of British Cassis and the smoothness of Chase Vodka go a long way in helping me do this, all I need to do is choose the right spirits and mixers, get the right balance and I have stunning cocktails to serve my guests. Almost every cocktail I serve, I taste – not a bad job!" **Joe Williams**

Poire Sour

Serves: **1**
- 50ml (2fl oz) of British Poire
- 25ml (1fl oz) Chase Rhubarb Vodka
- Juice of half a lemon
- 10-15ml (½fl oz) sugar syrup

1 Squeeze the juice from the lemon in to a 'Rocks' glass, add roughly the same amount of sugar syrup and stir so it mixes.

2 Next add the British Poire and continue stirring. Once mixed fill the glass with crushed ice cubes and drizzle the Chase Rhubarb over the top.

Chase Distillery

"Family-owned Chase Distillery is housed in a converted hop kiln barn nestled amongst 400 acres of Herefordshire farmland. From rolling potato fields to sweet-smelling apple orchards, it's here that we turn our organically grown produce from the Chase farm, into our award winning single estate vodka and gin. The highly skilled, artisanal distillation process adapts traditional methods not changed since the 1900's. Using a bespoke copper batch pot, Europe's tallest rectification tower (standing at 70ft), and our beautiful Carter Head style still, 'Ginny', each lovingly crafted bottle also remains hand-filled and sealed on site, ensuring a truly single-estate process from field to bottle." **William Chase**

Kiss Chase Cocktail

1 Half fill a highball glass with ice. Pour in the Chase vodka and Chase elderflower liqueur. Stir to mix.

2 Squeeze the juice from one lemon wedge into the glass and rub the lemon around the rim. Top the drink up with the apple juice and garnish with a lemon wedge.

Serves: 1
- 25ml (1fl oz) Chase vodka
- 25ml (1fl oz) Chase elderflower liqueur
- 2 lemon wedges
- Cloudy apple juice (to top up)

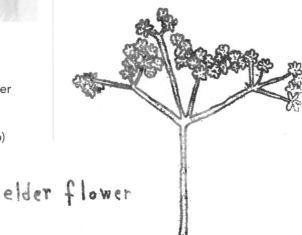

elder flower

Herefordshire Food Links

"Herefordshire Food Links was established in 2006 to bring together all those interested in local food across Herefordshire. Principally a network and directory of food businesses, with a focus on small to medium sized businesses, Food Links continues to promote local food to consumers and other end users, such as schools, other public sector organisations, and hotels and restaurants. Food Links is supported and managed by the Bulmer Foundation, an independent sustainable development charity core funded by Heineken UK. The Bulmer Foundation is also a founding member of the Herefordshire Food and Drink Partnership, a multi agency partnership who published the Sustainable Food and Drink Strategy for Herefordshire: a plan that aims to meet the challenges of securing our food supply now and into the future." **Peter Norton**

Elderflower Cordial

Makes: **1 litre**
- 20 elderflower heads (pick on a dry day when the flowers are just beginning to open)
- 3 lemons
- 25g (1oz) citric acid
- 1kg (2lbs 3oz) sugar
- 1 litre (1¾ pints) water

1 Boil the water, place the sugar in a large bowl and pour on the boiling water. Stir to dissolve. Grate the rind of the lemons in then slice and add the fruit. Add the citric acid and the flower heads.

2 Leave for 24 hours, stirring occasionally. Sieve through muslin, pour into clean sterilised bottles and seal. Keeps for up to 6 months or can be frozen in plastic bottles, leaving room for expansion.

To serve, dilute with still or sparkling water, over ice.

Herefordshire's fertile landscape lends itself to wild food as much as it does to cultivation. In fact the word 'foray' as a term to denote mushroom foraging derives from the original Woolhope Naturalists Field Club events of the same name. Although safely identifying mushrooms can be problematic there is an abundance of more easily recognisable food to be had, particularly from the hedgerows, which are an important landscape feature and habitat supporting wildlife and bio-diversity. Perhaps the most obvious is the blackberry, for which there is said to be over 40 varieties, however Herefordshire also has a tradition of growing damson hedgerows and the elder tree can be found almost everywhere offering up both flowers in spring and berries in autumn for our consumption.

time for tea...

Directory

Ballingham Hall Farm
Quality beef and lamb reared on our farm in the beautiful Herefordshire countryside.
www.castlehse.co.uk
george.watkins@castlehse.co.uk
01432 356321
Ballingham Hall, Hereford, HR2 6NH

Bearwood Bees
Honey made by happy bees in Herefordshire.
www.bearwoodbees.co.uk
info@bearwoodbees.co.uk
01544 388302
Hopleys, Bearwood, Pembridge, HR6 9EQ

Betty Twyford
A vintage inspired company with a focus on the home and family.
www.bettytwyford.com
sales@bettytwyford.com
01568 611124
C3-C5 Marches Trade Park, Brunel Road,
Leominster Enterprise Park, Leominster, HR6 0LX

Brinsop Court Estate
Luxury self catering accommodation in historic surroundings for reunions, relaxation and romance.
www.brinsopcourt.com
enquiries@brinsopcourt.com
01432 509925
Estate Office, Brinsop Court Estate, Brinsop, HR4 7AX

British Cassis
Award winning alcoholic fruit mixers, made on our family farm.
www.britishcassis.co.uk
info@britishcassis.co.uk
01544 340241
Whittern Farms Ltd, Lyonshall, HR5 3JA

Broadfield Court & Bodenham English Wines
Busy gardens and café open daily, serving fresh produce and own grown wine.
www.broadfieldcourt.co.uk
info@broadfieldcourt.co.uk
01568 797483
Bowley Lane, Bodenham, HR1 3LG

Brockmanton Rapeseed Oil
Cold pressed rapeseed oil.
www.brockmantonoils.co.uk
ryan@brockmantonoils.co.uk
01568 760966 / 07836 577802
Brockmanton Hall, Pudleston, Leominster, HR6 0QU

Bulmers Cider
Premium British bottled cider.
www.bulmers.com
01432 352000
The Cider Mill, Plough Lane, Hereford, HR4 0LE

Burton Court
Historic family run manor for unique weddings and corporate events.
www.burtoncourt.com
info@burtoncourt.com
01544 388222
Eardisland, Nr Leominster, HR6 9DN

Café @ All Saints
Homemade food in stunning re-ordered church in Hereford city centre.
www.cafeatallsaints.co.uk
manager@cafeatallsaints.co.uk
01432 370415
All Saints Church, High Street, Hereford, HR4 9AA

Cargill
Cargill's Hereford site produces chicken products for retail and food service markets.
www.cargill.co.uk
information_cme@cargill.com
01432 362000
Grandstand Road, Hereford, HR4 9PB

Castle Brook Vineyard
English sparking wine.
www.castle-brook.co.uk
office@cobrey.co.uk
01989 562770
Castle Brook Vineyard, Coleraine Buildings, Coughton,
Ross-on-Wye, HR9 5SG

Castle House
A unique privately owned boutique townhouse hotel
with an award-winning two rosette restaurant.
www.castlehse.co.uk
info@castlehse.co.uk
01432 356321
Castle House, Castle Street, Hereford, HR1 2NW

Celtic Vale Natural Mineral Water
The only officially recognised 'natural mineral water'
in Herefordshire.
www.celticvale.co.uk
info@celticvale.co.uk
01873 860295
Springvale, Longtown

Chase Distillery
The only independent, family run single-estate
distillery in the UK.
www.chasedistillery.co.uk
single-estate@williamchase.co.uk
01531 670049
Rosemaund Farm, Hereford, HR1 3PG

Church Barn Farm Shop
Family run farm shop, passionate about farming
and Herefordshire countryside.
www.churchbarnfarmshop.co.uk
info@churchbarnfarmshop.co.uk
01497 831414
Whitney on Wye, HR3 6EH

Cobrey Farms
Wye Valley asparagus.
www.cobrey.co.uk
office@cobrey.co.uk
01989 562770
Coughton, Ross-on-Wye, HR9 5SG

The Colloquy
A large and exclusive house in Herefordshire,
perfect for self catering luxury.
www.thecolloquy.com
info@thecolloquy.com
01544 340241
Lyonshall, HR5 3JA

Country Flavours Ltd
Suppliers of local free-range eggs, fresh from the farm.
www.country-flavours.co.uk
info@country-flavours.co.uk
01981 500005
Lower Bellamore, Preston-on-Wye, HR2 9JS

Court Farm & Leisure
Court Farm grow a huge range of fresh seasonal fruit
and vegetables.
www.courtfarmleisure.co.uk
courtfarmleisure@tiscali.co.uk
01432 760271
Tillington, HR4 8LG

The Courtyard Café Bar
Delicious food and an inspiring atmosphere in a quality venue.
www.courtyard.org.uk
catering@courtyard.org.uk
01432 346525
The Courtyard, Edgar Street, Hereford, HR4 9JR

The Crown Inn, Woolhope
Traditional village freehouse at the heart of Woolhope.
www.crowninnwoolhope.co.uk
matt@crowninnwoolhope.co.uk
01432 860468
Woolhope, HR1 4QP

Dewsall
A unique, idyllic hideaway for exclusive use and supper clubs.
www.dewsall.com
info@dewsall.com
01432 276724
Callow, Hereford, HR2 8DA

Frome Valley Vineyard
We produce white, sparkling and rose wines from crisp dry
to rounded medium.
www.fromewine.co.uk
01885 490768
Frome Valley Vineyards, Paunton Court, Bishops Frome, WR6 5BJ

The Garden Tea Room & Deli
Run by mother and son team from their vintage home in Kingsland.
www.thegardentearoom.co.uk
01568 709142
Stoneleigh, Kingsland, Leominster, HR6 9QS

Golden Valley Goats Ltd
Supplier of goat's milk, goat's cheese and goat meat.
www.goldenvalleygoats.co.uk
robandmim@btinternet.com
01981 251880
Cornerstone, Madley, HR2 9LP

The Great British Florist
Hand-tied, British grown flowers, scent with love.
www.greatbritishflorist.co.uk
flowers@greatbritishflorist.co.uk
01981 500930
Lower Blakemere Farm, Blakemere, Hereford, HR2 9PX

Gwatkin Cider
Traditional cider and perry from home-grown cider apples
and pears.
www.gwatkincider.co.uk
info@gwatkincider.co.uk
01981 550258
Moorhampton Park Farm, Abbey Dore, HR2 0AL

The Handmade Scotch Egg Co Ltd
Free range, handmade Scotch eggs with personality,
created with passion.
www.handmadescotcheggs.co.uk
info@handmadescotcheggs.co.uk
01885 490520
The Eggshed, Bishops Frome, WR6 5BT

Hedonist Bakery
Indulgent authentic recipes producing the finest range of
additive free handmade breads and pastries.
www.hedonistbakery.co.uk
info@hedonistbakery.co.uk
01989 741010
Hedonist Food Ltd, Ross-on-Wye, HR9 7TQ

Hereford Cathedral School
www.herefordcs.com
01432 363522
The Old Deanery, Cathedral Close, Hereford, HR1 2NG

Herefordshire Food Links
A network and directory of local food, bringing together
producers, processors, pubs and restaurants and consumers.
www.herefordshirefoodlinks.org.uk
www.bulmerfoundation.org.uk
info@bulmerfoundation.org.uk
01432 378409
The Cider Museum, 21 Ryelands Street, Hereford, HR4 0LW

Hopes of Longtown
Combining a diverse range of speciality and regional produce
with the practical facets of a convenience store.
www.hopesoflongtown.co.uk
info@hopesoflongtown.co.uk
01873 860444
The Farmers Barn, Longtown, HR2 0LT

James Moss at The Lakeside
Delicious food at our holiday home park bar and restaurant.
ejamesmoss@yahoo.co.uk
01568 709000
Pearl Lake Leisure Park, Shobdon, Leominster, HR6 9NQ

JJ Potatoes Ltd
Suppliers of quality chipping potatoes.
rhysefarm@gmail.com
01544 340619
Rhyse Villa, Lyonshall, Kington, HR5 3LX

John Lewis Fine Foods
The finest vegetables, fruits, dried goods and more,
delivered around Herefordshire.
www.johnlewisfinefoods.co.uk
johnlewisfinefoodsandwine@gmail.com
01989 567002
Unit 6 Thomas Row, Haigh Industrial Estate, Ross-on-Wye, HR9 5LB

Jus
Producing single variety apple juice.
www.jusapples.co.uk
enquiries@jusapples.co.uk
01531 670749
Birchley, Aylton, Ledbury, HR8 2QH

Just Rachel Quality Desserts
Top quality, award winning, luxury ice creams,
sorbets and desserts.
www.justrachel.com
info@justrachel.com
01531 650639
The Old Dairy, Churches Farm, Eggs Tump,
Bromsberrow, Nr Ledbury, HR8 1SA

The Kilpeck Inn
Warm, friendly service and top quality food sourced from
local suppliers.
www.kilpeckinn.com
enquiries@kilpeckinn.com
01981 570464
Hereford, HR2 9DN

Ledbury Real Ales
Award winning family run microbrewery who use local hops
for distinctive flavours.
www.ledburyrealales.co.uk
info@ledburyrealales.co.uk
01531 671184
Gazerdine House, Hereford Road, Ledbury, HR8 2PZ

Legges of Bromyard
Locally sourced meat and high class deli. Visit our shop
or buy online.
www.leggesofbromyard.com
info@leggesofbromyard.com
01885 482417
Tenbury Road, Bromyard, HR7 4LW

The Lion, Leintwardine
5 star country inn, stunning location, serving delicious
local food.
www.thelionleintwardine.co.uk
enquiries@thelionleintwardine.co.uk
01547 540203
High Street, Leintwardine, SY7 0JZ

Lodge Farm Kitchen
Convenient, tasty, nutritious meals made from fresh
ingredients, sourced locally.
www.lodgefarmkitchen.com
orders@lodgefarmkitchen.com
01989 764422
Deepdean, Ross-on-Wye, HR9 5SQ

Lower Buckton Country House (@agaqueen)
Country dinner, bed and breakfast stuffed with total,
local seasonal food!
www.lowerbuckton.co.uk
www.facebook.com/lowerbucktoncountryhouse
01547 540532 / 07960 273865
Buckton, Nr Leintwardine, SY7 0JU

Lower Hope Fruit
Fruit growers specialising in the production of sweet cherries.
www.lowerhopecherries.co.uk
admin@lowerhopefarms.co.uk
01432 820218
Lower Hope Farms, Ullingswick, Hereford, HR1 3JF

Lulham Court Vineyard
A three acre vineyard surrounded by the wonderful Wye Valley.
www.lulhamcourtvineyard.co.uk
enquiries@lulhamcourtvineyard.co.uk
01981 251107
Lulham Court, Lulham, Nr Madley, Hereford, HR2 9JQ

Mayfields Brewery
Herefordshire's best kept secret. Quietly converting people to our flavoursome beers.
www.mayfieldsbrewery.co.uk
info@mayfieldsbrewery.co.uk
01568 611197
8 Croft Business Park, Southern Ave, Leominster, HR6 0QF

The Mill Race
Contemporary village pub using local seasonal produce.
www.millrace.info
enquiries@millrace.info
01989 562891
Walford, Ross-on-Wye, HR9 5QS

Monkhide
Creating excellent drinks in our Herefordshire winery for the past 13 years.
www.monkhide.com
01432 839016
Carlton House, Canon Pyon, Hereford, HR4 8NY

Mousetrap Cheese
We specialise in the finest quality cheese, championing local artisan cheese makers.
www.mousetrapcheese.co.uk
info@mousetrapcheese.co.uk
01568 615512
The Mousetrap Cheese Shop, 30 Church Street, Hereford, HR1 2LR

Mycocoa
Delicious handmade chocolates with amazing flavours.
www.mycocoa.co.uk
info@mycocoa.co.uk
07717 119347

Neal's Yard Creamery
Makers of artisan goat's cheese, soft cow's cheese, yoghurt and creme fraîche.
www.nealsyardcreamery.co.uk
nealsyardcreamery@intamail.com
01981 500395
Caeperthy, Arthurs Stone Lane, Dorstone, Hereford, HR3 6AX

Neil Powell, Master Butchers
The finest locally sourced meats from Herefordshire and Monmouthshire.
www.masterbutchers.co.uk
ben.powell@masterbutchers.co.uk
01981 240000
Unit 1 Longmeadow Estate, Ewyas Harold, Hereford, HR2 0UA

Noke Lane Bakery
Small artisan bakery specialising in handmade breads and patisserie.
www.nokelanebakery.co.uk
info@nokelanebakery.co.uk
01544 387969
2 Noke Cottages, Noke Lane, Pembridge, HR6 9HW

Oliver's Cider & Perry
Real cider and perry in bottle and draught.
www.oliversciderandperry.co.uk
sales@oliversciderandperry.co.uk
07768 732026
The Old Hop Kilns, Moor House Farm, Ocle Pychard, HR1 3QZ

Once Upon A Tree Ltd
Producer of award winning Herefordshire cider, perry and apple juice.
www.onceuponatree.co.uk
info@onceuponatree.co.uk
01531 670263
Dragon Orchard, Putley, Ledbury, HR8 2RG

The Orgasmic Cider Co Ltd
Craft cider and perry makers.
www.orgasmiccidercompany.co.uk
orgasmic_cider@hotmail.co.uk
01544 327244 / 07773 037448
Great Parton, Eardisley, HR3 6NX

The Outdoor Kitchen
Importing enamel cookware from Hungary for outdoor kitchens and camp cooking.
www.outdoor-kitchen.biz
trish@maccurrach.com
07791 935955
Kington

Pengethley Farm Shop
'A taste of Herefordshire'. Locally grown and sourced fine foods.
www.pengethleyfarmshop.com
sale.pfs@btconnect.com
01989 730430
Peterstow, Ross-on-Wye, HR9 6LN

Pixley Berries
Juices and cordials made with lashings of fruit at our Herefordshire farm.
www.pixleyberries.co.uk
enquiries@pixleyberries.co.uk
01531 670228
Pixley Court, Pixley, Ledbury, HR8 2QA

Rayeesa's Indian Kitchen
Herefordshire's first and only authentic Indian cookery school.
www.rayeesasindiankitchen.com
info@rayeesasindiankitchen.com
01432 870253 / 07570 912922
Orchard Farmhouse, Mordiford, Hereford, HR1 4EJ

The Riverside Inn & Restaurant, Aymestrey
Pure Marches country-classic flavours in a Herefordshire style.
www.theriversideinn.org
theriverside@btconnect.com
01568 708440
Aymestrey, HR6 9ST

Rowlestone Farmhouse Ice cream
Farm made ice creams and sorbet.
www.rowlestonecourt.co.uk
info@rowlestonecourt.co.uk
01981 240322
Rowlestone Court, Rowlestone, Hereford, HR2 0DW

Saxtys
Independently owned bar, restaurant and club.
www.saxtys.co.uk
events@saxtys.co.uk
01432 357872
33 Widemarsh Street, Hereford, HR4 9EA

The Shack Revolution
Bringing you everything fun, fresh and British.
www.theshackrevolution.co.uk
rich@theshackrevolution.co.uk
01885 488325
The Shack HQ, Brickhouse Farm, Edwin Ralph, HR7 4LU

Shepherds Ice Cream
A gelato style ice cream made from sheep's milk.
www.shepherdsicecream.co.uk
enquiries@shepherdsicecream.co.uk
01981 550716
Cwm Farm, Peterchurch, Hereford, HR2 0TA

The Spiceworks (Hereford Herbs & Spices)
Stockists of dried herbs and spices from around the world.
www.thespiceworks.co.uk
info@thespiceworks.co.uk
01432 818666
28 Eign Gate, Hereford, HR4 0AB

The Stagg Inn at Titley
Michelin starred dining pub with accommodation.
www.thestagg.co.uk
reservations@thestagg.co.uk
01544 230221
Titley, Kington, HR5 3RL

Sue Gilmour Chocolates
Chocolate bars, shards and other chocolate goodies.
www.suegilmour.co.uk
sales@suegilmour.co.uk
01885 483132
The Old Rectory, Delamere Road, Tedstone, Delamere,
Bromyard, HR7 4QF

The Temple Bar Inn
Freehouse, with restaurant and 3 ensuite B&B rooms.
www.thetemplebarinn.co.uk
phillytemplebar@btinternet.com
01981 240423
Ewyas Harold, HR2 0EU

Tyrrells Potato Crisps
We make handcooked potato crisps from local
Herefordshire potatoes.
www.tyrrellscrisps.com
info@tyrrellscrisps.co.uk
01568 720 244
Tyrrells Court, Stretford Bridge, Leominster, HR6 9DQ

Upper Newton Farmhouse Accommodation
Herefordshire holiday accommodation at its best with slow
food and slow gardening.
www.herefordshireholidays.co.uk
pearl@herefordshireholidays.co.uk
01544 327727
Kinnersley, Hereford, HR3 6QB

Visit Herefordshire
Promoting and marketing our wonderful county nationally,
regionally and locally.
www.visitherefordshire.co.uk
www.flavoursofherefordshire.co.uk
enquiries@visitherefordshire.co.uk
01432 268430
The Discover Herefordshire Centre, 1 King Street,
Hereford, HR4 9BW

Watercress Harrys
Independent cocktail lounge bar.
www.watercressharrys.co.uk
events@watercressharrys.co.uk
01432 270175
8 St Peters Street, Hereford, HR1 2LE

Weobley Ash
Producing mutton, hogget and lamb, eggs and apple produce.
www.weobleyash.co.uk
weobleyash1@gmail.com
01544 267684
Stansbatch, Leominster, HR6 9LW

H Weston & Sons Ltd
Producing refreshing cider and perry from delicious
Herefordshire apples and pears since 1880.
www.westons-cider.co.uk
enquiries@westons-cider.co.uk
01531 660233
The Bounds, Much Marcle, Ledbury, HR8 2NQ

Windmill Hill Fruits
Quality, award winning, nutritious frozen fruit range that is
100% British.
www.windmillhillfruits.co.uk
enquiries@windmillhillfruits.co.uk
01989 730229
Windmill Hill, Harewood End, Hereford, HR2 8JS

Wye Valley Brewery
Regional brewery dedicated to brewing the best quality cask
conditioned beer.
www.wyevalleybrewery.co.uk
marketing@wyevalleybrewery.co.uk
01885 490505
Stoke Lacy, HR7 4HG

Wye Valley Granola
A delicious healthy artisan cereal made of oats, seeds and nuts.
www.wyevalleygranola.co.uk
angharad@wyevalleygranola.co.uk
07958 459858
Palmerston Road, Ross-on-Wye, HR9 5PN

Ye Olde Steppes – Pembridge Shop & Tearoom
Interesting and unusual traditional village shop and
vintage tearoom.
www.yeoldesteppes.co.uk
yeoldesteppes@gmail.com
01544 388506
High Street, Pembridge, HR6 9DS

A little mention

Special thanks go to...
Jo Hilditch, our sponsor, project manager, editor and all round angel – without you this project would not be the success it is.

Duchy of Cornwall whose generous sponsorship to our project has allowed two additional contributors to participate.

Stephen Wild and Pearl Taylor for their eagle eyes.

Betty Twyford for lending us super props.
www.bettytwyford.com

Recipe credits
Oliver's Mussel Gratin
by Lindy Wildsmith www.lindywildsmith.co.uk

Potato Blinis
by Andy Link at The Riverside Inn www.theriversideinn.org

Duck and Walnut Salad with Blackcurrants
by James Moss at the Lakeside

Roasted Fillet of Herefordshire Beef, Oxtail Hash Croquettes, Stewed Prunes and Ledbury Dark Gravy
by Callum McDonald in association with Ledbury Real Ales

Pork, Apricot and Orgasmic Cider Pie with Black Pudding Mash and Baby Leeks
by The Sun Inn at Winforton www.thesuninnwinforton.co.uk

Cherry Clafoutis
by Isabel Roper – Izzie's Catering www.flanesfordpriory.co.uk/izzies-catering

BV Stout and Rose Tiramisu
by Liz Knight www.foragefinefoods.co.uk

fork   knife   spoon